Learn Latin with Beginner Stories - De Viris Illustribus

HypLern Interlinear Project
www.hyplern.com

First edition: 2025, September

Author: Anonymous
Translation: Dr Th. van den End
Foreword: Camilo Andrés Bonilla Carvajal PhD

ISBN: 978-1-988830-69-8

kees@hyplern.com
www.hyplern.com

Learn Latin with Beginner Stories - De Viris Illustribus

Interlinear Latin to English

Author
Anonymous

Translation
Dr Th. van den End

HypLern Interlinear Project
www.hyplern.com

The HypLern Method

Learning a foreign language should not mean leafing through page after page in a bilingual dictionary until one's fingertips begin to hurt. Quite the contrary, through everyday language use, friendly reading, and direct exposure to the language we can get well on our way towards mastery of the vocabulary and grammar needed to read native texts. In this manner, learners can be successful in the foreign language without too much study of grammar paradigms or rules. Indeed, Seneca expresses in his sixth epistle that "Longum iter est per praecepta, breve et efficax per exempla[1]."

The HypLern series constitutes an effort to provide a highly effective tool for experiential foreign language learning. Those who are genuinely interested in utilizing original literary works to learn a foreign language do not have to use conventional graded texts or adapted versions for novice readers. The former only distort the actual essence of literary works, while the latter are highly reduced in vocabulary and relevant content. This collection aims to bring the lively experience of reading stories as directly told by their very authors to foreign language learners.

Most excited adult language learners will at some point seek their teachers' guidance on the process of learning to read in the foreign language rather than seeking out external opinions. However, both teachers and learners lack a general reading technique or strategy. Oftentimes, students undertake the reading task equipped with nothing more than a bilingual dictionary, a grammar book, and lots of courage. These efforts often end in frustration as the student builds mis-constructed nonsensical sentences after many hours spent on an aimless translation drill.

Consequently, we have decided to develop this series of interlinear translations intended to afford a comprehensive edition of unabridged texts. These texts are presented as they were originally written with no changes in word choice or order. As a result, we have a translated piece conveying the true meaning under every word from the original work. Our readers receive then two books in just one volume: the original version and its translation.

The reading task is no longer a laborious exercise of patiently decoding unclear and seemingly complex paragraphs. What's more, reading becomes an enjoyable and meaningful process of cultural, philosophical and linguistic learning. Independent learners can then acquire expressions and vocabulary while understanding pragmatic and socio-cultural dimensions of the target language by reading in it rather than reading about it.

Our proposal, however, does not claim to be a novelty. Interlinear translation is as old as the Spanish tongue, e.g. "glosses of [Saint] Emilianus", interlinear bibles in Old German, and of course James Hamilton's work in the 1800s. About the latter, we remind the readers, that as a revolutionary freethinker he promoted the publication of Greco-Roman classic works and further pieces in diverse languages. His effort, such as ours, sought to lighten the exhausting task of looking words up in large glossaries as an educational practice: "if there is any thing which fills reflecting men with melancholy and regret, it is the waste of mortal time, parental money, and puerile happiness, in the present method of pursuing Latin and Greek[2]".

Additionally, another influential figure in the same line of thought as Hamilton was John Locke. Locke was also the philosopher and translator of the Fabulae AEsopi in an interlinear plan. In 1600, he was already suggesting that interlinear texts, everyday communication, and use of the target language could be the most appropriate ways to achieve language learning:

> ...the true and genuine Way, and that which I would propose, not only as the easiest and best, wherein a Child might, without pains or Chiding, get a Language which others are wont to be whipt for at School six or seven Years together...[3]

---

1   "The journey is long through precepts, but brief and effective through examples". Seneca, Lucius Annaeus. (1961) Ad Lucilium Epistulae Morales, vol. I. London: W. Heinemann.

2   In: Hamilton, James (1829?) History, principles, practice and results of the Hamiltonian system, with answers to the Edinburgh and Westminster reviews; A lecture delivered at Liverpool; and instructions for the use of the books published on the system. Londres: W. Aylott and Co., 8, Pater Noster Row. p. 29.

3   In: Locke, John. (1693) Some thoughts concerning education. Londres: A. and J. Churchill. pp. 196-7.

Who can benefit from this edition?

We identify three kinds of readers, namely, those who take this work as a search tool, those who want to learn a language by reading authentic materials, and those attempting to read writers in their original language. The HypLern collection constitutes a very effective instrument for all of them.

1. For the first target audience, this edition represents a search tool to connect their mother tongue with that of the writer's. Therefore, they have the opportunity to read over an original literary work in an enriching and certain manner.
2. For the second group, reading every word or idiomatic expression in its actual context of use will yield a strong association between the form, the collocation, and the context. This will have a direct impact on long term learning of passive vocabulary, gradually building genuine reading ability in the original language. This book is an ideal companion not only to independent learners but also to those who take lessons with a teacher. At the same time, the continuous feeling of achievement produced during the process of reading original authors both stimulates and empowers the learner to study[1].
3. Finally, the third kind of reader will notice the same benefits as the previous ones. The proximity of a word and its translation in our interlinear texts is a step further from other collections, such as the Loeb Classical Library. Although their works might be considered the most famous in this genre, the presentation of texts on opposite pages hinders the immediate link between words and their semantic equivalence in our native tongue (or one we have a strong mastery of).

---

1 Some further ways of using the present work include:

1. As you progress through the stories, focus less on the lower line (the English translation). Instead, try to read through the upper line, staying in the foreign language as long as possible.
2. Even if you find glosses or explanatory footnotes about the mechanics of the language, you should make your own hypotheses on word formation and syntactical functions in a sentence. Feel confident about inferring your own language rules and test them progressively. You can also take notes concerning those idiomatic expressions or special language usage that calls your attention for later study.
3. As soon as you finish each text, check the reading in the original version (with no interlinear or parallel translation). This will fulfil the main goal of this

collection: bridging the gap between readers and original literary works, training them to read directly and independently.

Why interlinear?

Conventionally speaking, tiresome reading in tricky and exhausting circumstances has been the common definition of learning by texts. This collection offers a friendly reading format where the language is not a stumbling block anymore. Contrastively, our collection presents a language as a vehicle through which readers can attain and understand their authors' written ideas.

While learning to read, most people are urged to use the dictionary and distinguish words from multiple entries. We help readers skip this step by providing the proper translation based on the surrounding context. In so doing, readers have the chance to invest energy and time in understanding the text and learning vocabulary; they read quickly and easily like a skilled horseman cantering through a book.

Thereby we stress the fact that our proposal is not new at all. Others have tried the same before, coming up with evident and substantial outcomes. Certainly, we are not pioneers in designing interlinear texts. Nonetheless, we are nowadays the only, and doubtless, the best, in providing you with interlinear foreign language texts.

Handling instructions

Using this book is very easy. Each text should be read at least three times in order to explore the whole potential of the method. The first phase is devoted to comparing words in the foreign language to those in the mother tongue. This is to say, the upper line is contrasted to the lower line as the following example shows:

CAII	FABRICII	VIRTUS
of Caius	Fabricius	the courage

The second phase of reading focuses on capturing the meaning and sense of the original text. As readers gain practice with the method, they should be able to focus on the target language without getting distracted by the translation. New users of the method, however, may find it helpful to cover the translated lines with a piece of paper as illustrated in the image below. Subsequently, they try to understand the meaning of every word, phrase, and entire sentences in the target language itself, drawing on the translation only when necessary. In this phase, the reader should resist the temptation to look at the translation for every word. In doing so, they will find that they are able to understand a good portion of the text by reading directly in the target language, without the crutch of the translation. This is the skill we are looking to train: the ability to read and understand native materials and enjoy them as native speakers do, that being, directly in the original language.

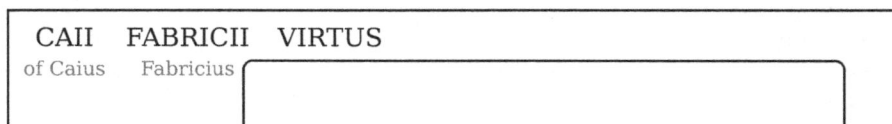

CAII   FABRICII   VIRTUS
of Caius   Fabricius

In the final phase, readers will be able to understand the meaning of the text when reading it without additional help. There may be some less common words and phrases which have not cemented themselves yet in the reader's brain, but the majority of the story should not pose any problems. If desired, the reader can use an SRS or some other memorization method to learning these straggling words.

CAII FABRICII VIRTUS

Above all, readers will not have to look every word up in a dictionary to read a text in the foreign language. This otherwise wasted time will be spent concentrating on their principal interest. These new readers will tackle authentic texts while learning their vocabulary and expressions to use in further communicative (written or oral) situations. This book is just one work from an overall series with the same purpose. It really helps those who are afraid of having "poor vocabulary" to feel confident about reading directly in the language. To all of them and to all of you, welcome to the amazing experience of living a foreign language!

Additional tools

Check out shop.hyplern.com or contact us at info@hyplern.com for free mp3s (if available) and free empty (untranslated) versions of the eBooks that we have on offer.

For some of the older eBooks and paperbacks we have Windows, iOS and Android apps available that, next to the interlinear format, allow for a pop-up format, where hovering over a word or clicking on it gives you its meaning. The apps also have any mp3s, if available, and integrated vocabulary practice.

Visit the site hyplern.com for the same functionality online. This is where we will be working non-stop to make all our material available in multiple formats, including audio where available, and vocabulary practice.

Table of Contents

Chapter I

ROMANI **IMPERII** **EXORDIUM:** **ROMULUS** **ET**
Of the Roman   Empire   The beginnings   Romulus   and

REMUS
Remus

Proca, **rex** **Albanorum,** **duos** **filios,** **Numitorem** **et**
Proca   king   of the Albani   two   sons   Numitor   and
                                {duo4}

Amulium **habuit.** **Numitori,** **qui** **natu** **maior** **erat,**
Amulius   had   To Numitor   who   by birth   greater   was
           {pf}   (older)

regnum **reliquit;** **sed** **Amulius,** **pulso**
the kingdom   he left   but   Amulius   having driven out
               {pf}

fratre, **regnavit,** **et** **ut** **eum** **sobole**
(his) brother   reigned   and   in order that   him   of offspring
                 {pf}

privaret, **Rheam** **Sylviam** **eius** **filiam** **Vestae**
he would rob   Rhea   Sylvia   his   daughter   of Vesta

sacerdotem **fecit,** **quae** **tamen** **Romulum** **et**
a priestess   he made   who   however   Romulus   and
               {pf}

Remumuno partu edidit. Quo cognito,
Remus in one childbirth produced What having been known
{pf} (This)

Amulius ipsam in vincula coniecit, parvulos
Amulius her in chains threw the little ones
(prison) {pf}

alveo impositos abiecit in Tiberim, qui
in a bucket having been put threw away into the Tiber which
{pf}

tunc forte super ripas erat effusus; sed,
then strongly over the banks was overflowed but
(beyond) (had)

relabente flumine, eos aqua in sicco reliquit.
falling back the river them the water in the dry left
(on) {pf}

Vastae tum in eis locis solitudines erant.
Vast then in those places wildernesses (there) were

Lupa, ut fama traditum est, ad vagitum
A she-wolf as by rumor handed down is to the crying

accurrit, infantes lingua lambit, ubera
has run the children with (her) tongue licked (her) udders
(ran)

eorum ori admovit, matremque se gessit.
of them mouth moved to and (as) a mother herself behaved
{os3} {pf} {pf gero}

3

Cum	lupa	saepius	ad	parvulos	veluti	ad
When	the she-wolf	more often	to	the little ones	as if	to

catulos	reverteretur,	Faustulus,	pastor	regius,
puppies	came back	Faustulus	the herdsman	royal

rem	animadvertit,	eos	tulit	in	casam	et
the thing	noticed {pf}	them	brought {pf fero}	into	(his) house	and

Accae	Laurentiae	coniugi	dedit	educandos.	Qui
to Acca	Laurentia	(his) wife	gave {pf}	to bring up	Who (And they)

adulti	inter	pastores	primo	ludicris
having grown up	among	the herdsmen	at first	in playful

certaminibus	vires	auxere,	deinde,	venando
contests	(their) strength {vis4pl}	to increase	next	for hunting

saltus	peragrare	coeperunt,	tum	latrones	a
the woodlands	to wander in	began {pf}	then	the brigands	from

rapina	pecorum	arcere.	Quare	eis	insidiati
the robbing	of the sheep	to hinder	Wherefore	them	ambushed

sunt	latrones,	a	quibus	Remus	captus	est.
are (have)	the brigands	by	whom	Remus	caught	is (was)

Romulus autem vi se defendit. Tunc
Romulus however by (his) strength himself defended Then
{pf}

Faustulus necessitate compulsus indicavit Romulo
Faustulus by necessity compelled announced to Romulus
{pf}

quis esset eius avus, quae mater. Romulus
who was his grandfather who (his) mother Romulus

statim, armatis pastoribus Albam properavit.
at once having armed the herdsmen to Alba hurried
{pf}

Interea Remum latrones ad Amulium regem
In the meantime Remus the brigands to Amulius the king

perduxerunt, eum accusantes, quasi Numitoris
led him accusing as if of Numitor
{pf perduco}

greges infestare solitus esset; Remus itaque a
the herds to harass accustomed were Remus therefore by

rege Numitori ad supplicium traditus est: at
king Numitor to punishment handed over is But
(for) (was)

Numitor, considerato adolescentis vultu,
Numitor having observed or the youth the face
{vultus5}

haud procul erat quin nepotem agnosceret.
not far(nearly) was that not (his) grandson he would recognize

Nam Remus oris lineamentis erat matri
For Remus of the mouth the features(facial features) was to the mother

simillimus, aetasque tempori expositionis
very similar and his age (with) the time of the exposing

congruebat. Dum ea res animum Numitoris
corresponded While that matter the mind of Numitor

anxium teneret, repente Romulus supervenit,
anxious held(kept in fear) suddenly Romulus came up

fratrem liberavit, et Amulio interfecto,
(his) brother he freed {pf} and Amulius having been killed

avum Numitorem in regnum restituit.
(his) grandfather Numitor in the kingdom reinstated {pf}

Deinde Romulus et Remus urbem in eisdem
Thereupon (by) Romulus and Remus a town in the same

locis ubi expositi educatique fuerant
places where exposed and brought up they had been

condiderunt; **sed** **orta** **est** **inter** **eos** **contentio**
founded — but — arisen — is (has) — between — them — dispute

uter **nomen** **novae** **urbi** **daret,** **eamque**
who of both — the name — to the new — town {urbs3} — would give — and her

regeret; **adhibuerunt** **auspicia.** **Remus** **prior** **sex**
would rule — they consulted {pf} — auspices — Remus — earlier — six

vultures, **Romulus** **postea,** **sed** **duodecim,** **vidit.** **Sic**
vultures — Romulus — later — but — twelve — saw {pf} — Thus

Romulus **augurio** **victor** **Romam** **vocavit;** **et**
Romulus — by the sign — victor — Rome — named {pf} — and

ut **eam** **prius** **legibus** **quam** **moenibus**
in order that — her — earlier — with laws — than — with walls

muniret, **edixit** **ne** **quis** **vallum**
he would fortify — he proclaimed {pf edico} — that not — anybody — the wall

transiliret. **Quod** **Remus** **irridens** **transilivit;** **eum**
should jump over — Which (But it) — Remus — mocking — jumped over — him

iratus **Romulus** **interfecit,** **his** **increpans**
angered — Romulus — has slain — with these — scolding (him)

verbis: "Sic deinceps malo afficietur quicumque
words Thus hereafter by evil will be afflicted whoever
{malum5}

transiliet moenia mea." Ita solus potitus est
will jump over walls my In this way alone obtained is
(has)

imperio Romulus.
supreme power Romulus

Chapter II

ROMULUS, ROMANORUM REX PRIMUS. RAPTUS
Romulus of the Romans the king first The seizing

SABINARUM VIRGINUM
of the Sabine virgins

Romulus imaginem urbis magis quam urbem
Romulus likeness of a town more than a town
(rather)

fecerat. Deerant incolae. Erat in proximo
had made Lacked inhabitants There was in the neighbourhood
a match

lucus: hunc asylum fecit. Eo statim
a grove this place of refuge he made To it immediately
{hic4} {pf facio}

multitudo latronum pastorumque confugit. Cum
a multitude of brigands and herdsmen took refuge Because
{pf}

vero ipse et populus uxores non haberent,
but he himself and the people wives not had

9

legatos ad vicinas gentes misit, qui societatem
envoys to neighbouring peoples he sent who alliance
{pf mitto}

connumbiumque peterent. Nusquam benigne
and (inter)marriage should ask for In no place with benevolence

legatio audita est: ludibrium etiam additum:
the embassy heard is mockery also (was) added
(was)

"Quidni feminis quoque asylum aperuistis?
Why not for women also a place of refuge you have opened

Id enim compar foret connubium." Romulus
That for on equal terms would be a marriage Romulus
a match a match

aegritudinem animi dissimulans ludos parat:
aggrievement of (his) mind concealing games prepares

indici deinde finitimis spectaculum
to be announced thereupon to the neighbours a show

iubet. Multi convenerunt studio etiam
he orders Many gathered by eagerness also
{pf}

videndae novae urbis, maxime Sabini cum liberis
to see he new town mostly the Sabines with children

et coniugibus. Ubi spectaculi tempus venit,
and spouses Where of the spectacle the time came{pf}
(When)

eoque deditae mentes cum oculis erant,
and to it were given the minds together with the eyes were
(directed)

tum, dato signo, virgines raptae sunt: et
then having been given a sign the maidens seized are and
(were)

haec fuit statim causa bellorum.
this was immediately a cause of wars
{pf esse}

Sabini ob virgines raptas bellum adversus
The Sabines because of the maidens seized war against

Romanos sumpserunt, et cum Romae
the Romas took up and when Rome
(waged)

appropinquarent, Tarpeiam virginem nacti sunt,
they came near Tarpeia a maiden encountered are
{pf nanciscor} (have)

quae aquae causa sacrorum
who water{aqua2} for the matter of religious ceremonies

hauriendae descenderat. Huius pater
to draw had gone down Of whom father
(Her)

Romanae praeerat arci. Titus Tatius
to the Roman was in command citadel Titus Tatius
was in command of the citadel

Sabinorum dux Tarpeiae optionem muneris
of the Sabines the leader to Tarpeia the choice of a reward

dedit, si exercitum suum in Capitolium
gave if army his into the Capitol(ine hill)
{pf}

perduxisset. Illa petiit quod Sabini in
she would have led She requested that what the Sabines in
{pf} (at)

sinistris manibus gerebant, videlicet annulos et
the left hands wore that is to say the rings and

armillas. Quibus dolose promissis, Tarpeia
the bracelets These deceitfully having been promised Tarpeia

Sabinos in arcem perduxit, ubi Tatius eam
the Sabines into the citadel led where Tatius her
{pf perduco}

scutis obrui praecepit. Nam et
with the shields to be overwhelmed ordered For and
{pf} (too)

scuta in laevis habuerant. Sic impia
the shields in the left hand they had In this way wicked
{pf}

proditio **celeri** **poena** **vindicata est.**
the betrayal with a swift punishment avenged is
(was)

Romulus adversus Tatium processit, et in eo loco
Romulus against Tatius advanced and in that place
{pf procedo} (the)

ubi nunc Romanum forum est pugnam conseruit.
where now the Roman forum is battle joined
{pf}

Primo impetu, vir inter Romanos insignis,
In the first onslaught a man among the Romans outstanding

nomine Hostilius fortissime dimicans cecidit; cuius
by name Hostilius very strongly fighting fell whose
{pf cado}

interitu consternati Romani fugere coeperunt.
by death dismayed the Romans to flee have begun

Iam Sabini clamitabant: "Vicimus perfidos
Already the Sabines shouted We have won (the) perfidious
(We defeated)

hospites, imbelles hostes. Nunc sciunt longe
hosts unwarlike enemies Now they know by far

aliud esse virgines rapere, aliud pugnare
else to be maidens to seize something else to battle
(different)

cum viris." Tunc Romulus arma ad caelum tollens
with men Then Romulus (his) arms to the sky raising

Iovi aedem vovit, et exercitus seu forte
to Iupiter a temple vowed and the army either by chance
{pf voveo}

seu divinitus restitit. Proelium itaque
or in a divine way stood firm The battle thus
{pf resto}

redintegratur: sed raptae mulieres, crinibus
was restored but the seized women with hairs

passis, ausae sunt se inter tela
loosened dared are themselves between the spears
{ptps pando} (have)

volantia inferre; et hinc patres, inde viros
flying to insert and hence with fathers then with men

deprecatae, pacem conciliarunt.
entreating peace brought about

Romulus cum Tatio foedus percussit, et Sabinos
Romulus with Tatius a treaty struck and the Sabines
(concluded)

in urbem recepit. Centum ex senioribus
into the town received One hundred out of the elders
{pf}

elegit   quorum   consilio   omnia   ageret.
he chose   of whom   with the counsel   all things   he would conduct
{pf}

Ei   ob   senilem   aetatem   Senatus   vocati   sunt.
They   because of   (their) old   age   "Senate"   named   are

Tres   equitum   centurias   constituit;   plebem
Three   of "equites"   "centuriae"   he established   the (lower) people
{pf}

in   tringinta   curias   distribuit.   His   ita
in   thirty   "curiae"   he divided   These things   thus
{pf}

ordinatis,   cum   ad   Caprae   paludem
having been put in order   when   at   the Goats   Swamp
(on)

exercitum   lustraret,   subito   coorta   est   tempestas
the army   he reviewed   suddenly   come op   is   a storm
(has)

cum   magno   fragore   tonitribusque,   et   Romulus   e
with   great   crashing   and thunderbolts   and   Romulus   from

conspectu   ablatus   est: eum   ad
view   been carried away   is   him   to
(has)   that he had gone away

Deos   abiisse   vulgo   creditum   est;
the gods   to have gone away   by the pleople   believed   is
that he had gone away

cui rei fidem fecit Proculus vir nobilis.
to which -thing- faith made Proculus a man noble
{pf}

Orta enim inter patres et plebem
Having arisen for between the Fathers and the (lower) people

seditione, is in concionem processit, et
discord he into the meeting has come and

iureiurando affirmavit Romulum a se visum
with an oath has affirmed Romulus by him had been seen

augustiore forma quam fuisset, eumdemque
in a more august shape than he had been and the same one

praecipere ut seditionibus abstinerent, et
(had) ordered that from dissensions they would hold back and

virtutem colerent. Ita Romulus pro Deo cultus,
virtue would cultivate Thus Romulus as a god is revered

et Quirinus est appellatus.
and Quirinus is named

Chapter III

————

TULLUS HOSTILIUS, ROMANORUM REX TERTIUS.
Tullus   Hostilius   of the Romans   king   third

HORATIORUM ET CURIATIORUM CERTAMEN
of the Horatii   and   the Curiatii   combat

Mortuo   Numa,   Tullus   Hostilius   rex   creatus   est.
Having died   Numa   Tullus   Hostilius   king   been created (made)   is (has)

Hic   non   solum   proximo   regi   dissimilis,   sed
This one (He)   not   alone   to the nearest (last)   king   unlike   but

etiam   Romulo   ferocior   fuit.   Eo   regnante,
also   than Romulus   more fierce   was {pf}   Him   ruling / During his reign

bellum   inter   Albanos   et   Romanos   exortum   est.
a war   between   the Albani   and   the Romans   started   is (has)

Ducibus   Hostilio   et   Fuffetio   placuit,   paucorum
To the leaders   Hostilius   and   Fuffetius   pleased {pf}   of few

manibus **fata** **utriusque** **populi** **committi.**
to the hands / the fate / of both / people (peoples) / to commit

Erant **apud** **Romanos** **trigemini** **Horatii,**
(There) were / at (among) / the Romans / triplets / "the Horatii"

trigemini **quoque** **apud** **Albanos** **Curiatii.** **Cum** **eis**
triplets / also / at (among) / the Albani / "the Curiatii" / With / these

agunt **reges** **ut** **pro** **sua** **quisque** **patria**
act (arrrange) / the kings / that / for / his own / each / home town

dimicent **ferro.** **Foedus** **ictum** **est** **ea**
would combat / with iron/(armed) / An agreement / struck / is / with

lege, **ut** **unde** **victoria,** **ibi** **quoque**
this law (rule) / that / whence (where) / the victory / there / also

imperium **esset.** **Itaque** **trigemini** **arma**
the supreme power / would be / Thus / the triplets / the weapons

capiunt, **et** **in** **medium** **inter** **duas** **acies**
take up / and / in / the middle / between / the two / lines of battle

procedunt. **Consederant** **utrimque** **duo** **exercitus.**
advance / sat together / on each side / the two / armies

Datur signum, infestisque armis terni
is given   a sign   and with inimical   weapons   the three each
      (and with leveled)

iuvenes magnorum exercituum animos gerentes
young men   of large   armies   the spirits   carrying
      (courage)

concurrunt.
  clash

Ut primo concurso increpuere arma, horror
When   in the first   clash   resound   the arms   horror

ingens spectantes perstrinxit. Consertis
great   the onlookers   seized   Having joined
    {pf}   Having come to blows

deinde manibus, statim duo Romani alius
thereafter   the hands   at once   two   Romans   one
  Having come to blows

super alium expirantes ceciderunt: tres Albani
upon   the other   dying   fell   three   Albani
    {pf cado}

vulnerati. Ad casum Romanorum conclamavit
are wounded   At   the fall   of the Romans   cried out together
    {pf}

gaudio exercitus Albanus. Romanos iam spes tota
of joy   the army   Albanian   The Romans   already   hope   all

deserebat. **Unum** **Horatium** **tres** **Curiatii**
left (failed) / The one / Horatius / three / Curiatii

circumsteterant; **is** **quamvis** **integer,** **quia**
stood around {pf sto} / this one (he) / although / entire (unhurt) / because

tribus **impar** **erat,** **fugam** **simulavit,** **ut**
to three / not equal / he was / the flight / pretended {pf} / in order that

singulos **per** **intervalla** **secuturos** **separatim**
one by one / with / intervals / going to chase (him) / separately

aggrederetur. **Iam** **aliquantum** **spatii** **ex** **loco,**
he would attack. / Already / some / space (distance) / from / the place

ubi **pugnatum** **est,** **aufugerat,** **cum** **respiciens**
where / battled / is / he had fled away / `when / looking back

vidit **unum** **Curiatium** **haud** **procul** **ab** **se**
he saw {pf video} / one / of the Curiatii / not / far / from / himself

abesse. **In** **eum** **magno** **impetu** **redit** **et**
to be away / Towards / him / with a great / rush / he returns / and

dum **Albanus** **exercitus** **inclamat** **Curiatiis,** **ut** **opem**
while / the Alban / army / cries out to / the Curiatii / that / help

ferant	fratri,	iam	Horatius	eum
they bring	to (their) brother	already	Horatius	him

occiderat.	Alterum	deinde,	priusquam	tertius
had killed	The other one	thereafter	before	the third one

posset	consequi,	interfecit.
can	catch up	he has killed
		(he killed)

Iam	singuli	supererant	sed	nec	spe	nec
Already	one each	remained	but	not	in hope	nor

viribus	pares.	Alterius	erat	intactum	ferro
in strength	equal	Of the other	was	intact	by steel
		(one)		not injured	

corpus,	et	geminata	victoria	ferox	animus.
the body	and	the twinned	victory	fierce	the spirit
		(the repeated)			

Alter	fessum	vulnere,	fessum	cursu
The other one	exhausted	by (his) wound	exhausted	by running

trahebat	corpus.	Nec	illud	proelium	fuit.
dragged on	(his) body	And not	that	a fight	has been
					(was)

Romanus	exultans	male	sustinentem	arma
The Roman	exulting	(him) badly	holding up	(his) weapons
		(hardly)		

conficit,   iacentemque   spoliat.   Romani
finishes   and (him) laying down   robs (of his weaponry)   The Romans

ovantes   ac   gratulantes   Horatium   accipiunt,   et
cheering   and   congratulating   Horatius   receive   and

domum   deducunt.   Princeps   ibat   Horatius,
to (his) home   accompany (him)   In front   went   Horatius,

trium   fratrum   spolia   prae   se   gerens.   Cui
of three   brothers   the spoils   before   himself   carrying   To whom

obvia   fuit   soror,   quae   desponsa   fuerat
in the way   has been   (his) sister   who   pledged   had been
         (came)

uni   ex   Curiatiis.   Viso   super   humeros
to one   out of   the Curiatii   having been seen   upon   the shoulders
           {ablativus absolutus}

fratris   paludamento   sponsi,   quod   ipsa
of (her) brother   the cloak   of (her) fiancé   which   she herself
       {ablativus absolutus}

confecerat,   flere   et   crines   solvere   coepit.
had made   to weep   and   (her) hairs   to loosen   she began

Movit   feroci   iuveni   animum   comploratio
Stirred   fierce   to the young man   the mind   the loud complaint
{pf}

sororis	in	tanto	gaudio	publico.	Stricto
of (his) sister	in (amidst)	so great	a joy	public	with drawn

itaque	gladio	transfigit	puellam,	simul	eam
so	sword	he pierces	the girl	at the same time	her

verbis	increpans:	"Abi	hinc	cum
with the words	rebuking	Go away	from here	with

immaturo	amore	ad	sponsum;	oblita
immature	(your) love	to	(your) fiancé	having forgotten

fratrum,	oblita	patriae.	Sic	eat
(your) brothers	having forgotten	the home country	thus	may it go

quaecumque	Romana	lugebit	hostem."
to every (woman) who	Roman	will bewail	an enemy

Atrox	id	visum	est	facinus	patribus
Cruel	this	seemed	is	crime	to the (city) Fathers
	this crime has seemed				

plebique;	quare	raptus	est	in	ius
and the common people	for which matter	seized	is (was)	into	law

Horatius	et	apud	iudices	condemnatus.	Iam
Horatius	and	at (by)	the judges	condemned	Already

acesserat — had approached
lictor — the lictor
iniiciebatque — and threw (around his neck)
laqueum. — the noose

Tum — Then
Horatius — Horatius
ad — to
populum — the people
provocavit. — called out {pf}
Interea — In the meantime

pater — the father
Horatii — of Horatius
senex — old
proclamabat — proclaimed
filiam — daughter
suam — his

iure — lawfully
caesam — killed
fuisse; — to have been
et — and
iuvenem — the young man

amplexus, — having embraced
spoliaque — and the spoils
Curiatiorum — of the Curiatii
ostentans — showing

orabat — he begged
populum — the pleople
ne — that not
se — him
orbum — bereft
liberis — of children

faceret. — it would make
Non — Not
tulit — bore {pf}
populus — the people
patris — of the father
lacrymas, — the tears

iuvenemque — and the youth
absolvit, — it absolved {pf}
magis — more
admiratione — by admiration
virtutis, — of (his) courage

quam — than
iure — by the law / for the sake of the law
causae. — of the case
Ut — In order that
tamen — however
caedes — the murder

manifesta   expiaretur,   pater,   quibusdam
evident   would be expiated   the father   some

sacrificiis   peractis,   transmisit   per   viam
sacrifices   having been completed   put across   over   the street
                               {pf}

tigillum,   et   filium   capite   adoperto   velut   sub
a small beam   and   (his) son   with head   covered   as if   under

iugum   misit: quod   tigillum   sororium   appellatum
the yoke   he made go   which   beam   "the sister's"   named
              {pf}

est.
is

Non   diu   pax   Albana   mansit: nam   Fuffetius,
Not   a long time   the peace   Alban   remained   for   Fuffetius
                          (lasted)

dux   Albanorum,   cum   invidiosum   se   apud
the leader   of the Albans   because   odious   himself   at
                                  (among)

cives   videret   quod   bellum   uno   paucorum
the citizens   he saw   because   the war   by one   of few people
                              (by a)

certamine   finisset,   ut   rem
combat   had been ended   in order that   the matter

corrigeret, **Veientes** **adversus** **Romanos**
he would set right / the people of Veii / against / the Romans

concitavit. **Ipse** **ab** **Tullo** **in** **auxilium**
incited {pf} / He / by / Tullus / to / aid

arcessitus, **aciem** **in** **collem**
having been summoned / the line of battle (the army) / to / a hill

subduxit, **ut** **fortunam** **belli**
he stealthily led {pf} / in order that / the outcome / of the war

experiretur **ac** **sequeretur.** **Qua** **re**
he would find out / and / follow (observe) / Which / thing
After understanding that

Tullus **intellecta,** **dixit** **clara** **voce** **suo**
Tullus / having been understood / he said / clear / with a voice / on his
After understanding that / {pf}

illud **iussu** **Fuffetium** **facere,** **ut** **hostes** **a**
that / command / Fuffetius / to do (did) / so that / the enemies / from

tergo **circumvenirentur.** **Quo** **audito,**
the rear / he would circumvent / Which / having been heard

hostes **territi** **victique** **sunt.** **Postera** **die**
the enemies / frightened / and defeated / are (were) / On the next / day

Fuffetius **cum** **ad** **gratulandum** **Tulo** **venisset,**
Fuffetius · when · to · congratulate · Tullus · he had come

iussu **illius** **quadrigis** **religatus** **est,** **et** **in**
on the order · of him · to a chariot · bound · is (was) · and · in

diversa **distractus.** **Deinde** **Tullus** **Albam**
oppposite (directions) · drawn · Thereupon · Tullus · Alba

propter **ducis** **perfidiam** **diruit,** **et**
because of · its leader · the perfidy · destroyed {pf} · and

Albanos **Romam** **transire** **iussit.**
the people of Alba · to Rome · to go over · he commanded {pf iubeo}

Roma **interim** **crevit** **Albae** **ruinis.**
Rome · inn the meantime · grew {pf} · of Alba · by the downfall

Duplicatus **est** **civium** **numerus:** **mons** **Caelius**
doubled · is · of the citizens · the number · Mount · Caelius

urbi **additus,** **et** **quo** **frequentius**
to the town · was added · and · that it {ut eo} · more frequent (densely)

habitaretur, **eam** **sedem** **Tullus** **regiae**
would be inhabited · it · (as) seat · Tullus · of the royal palace

cepit, ibique deinde habitavit. Auctarum
has taken and there thereafter has resided in the augmented

virium fiducia elatus bellum Sabinis
forces by confidence Proud war on the Sabines
{vis2pl}

indixit. Pestilentia insecuta est. Nulla tamen
he declared A pest epidemy followed is no at all however
(has)

ab armis quies dabatur. Credebat enim rex
from arms rest was given believed For the king
(war)

bellicosus salubriora militiae quam domi esse
war-like more healthy in the military than at home to be

iuvenum corpora. Sed ipse quoque
of the young men the bodies But he himself also

diuturno morbo est implicitus: tunc fracti
by a long-lasting illness is implicated then broken
(struck)

simul cum corpore sunt spiritus illi feroces.
together with (his) body are minds those ferocious
(mind) (that)

Nullique rei deinceps nisi sacris operam
to no one thing thereafter if not to sacred matters labor
(save only) (attention)

dedit. **Memorant** **Tullum** **fulmine** **ictum**
he gave (People) recount Tullus by lightning struck
{pf do}

cum **domo** **conflagrasse.** **Tullus**
together with (his) house to have been consumed by fire Tullus

magna **gloria** **belli** **regnavit** **annos** **duos** **et**
with great glory of war ruled years two and
(martial) {pf}

triginta.
thirty

Chapter IV

TARQUINIUS **SUPERBUS,** **ROMANORUM** **REX**
Tarquinius Superbus of the Romans king

SEPTIMUS ET ULTIMUS
the seventh and last

Tarquinius **Superbus** **regnum** **sceleste**
Tarquinius "The Proud" the kingdom in a criminal way

occupavit. **Tamen** **bello** **strenuus** **hostes**
occupied However in war energetic the enemies

domuit. **Urbem** **Gabios** **in potestatem**
he has subdued The town Gabii in the power
under his authority

redegit **fraude** **Sexti** **filii.** **Is** **cum**
he brought back by the deceit of Sextus (his) son This one when

indigne ferret eam urbem a patre expugnari
unworthy he bore that town by (his) father be conquered
he was outraged

non posse, ad Gabinos se contulit,
not to be able (could) to the people of Gabii himself conveyed

patris in se saevitiam querens.
of (his) father towards himself the harshness complaining (about)

Benigne a Gabinis exceptus est, et paulatim
Kindly by the men of Gabii received he is and gradually

eorum benevolentiam fictis blanditiis
their favour with fictitious blandishments

alliciendo, dux belli electus est. Tum e
winning captain of war chosen he is (was) Then from among

suis unum ad patrem mittit sciscitatum
his own men one to (his) father he sent {pf} to get to know

quidnam se facere vellet. Pater nuntio
what him to do he wanted The father to the emissary

filii nihil respondit, sed in hortum transiit;
of (his) son nothing answered {pf} but into the garden went over {pf}

ibique inambulans, sequente nuntio,
and there walking up and down following the emissary with the envoy follwing him

altissima papaverum capita baculo decussit.
the highest of the poppies heads with (his) staff struck off
{pf decutio}

Nuntius fessus expectando redit Gabios. Sextus,
The emissary tired of waiting returned to Gabii Sextus
{pf}

cognito silentio patris simul ac
having known (that) the silence of (his) father at the same time and
at the same time also

facto, intellexit quid vellet pater.
(his) doing understood what wanted (his) father
{pf}

Primores civitatis interemit, patrique
The prominent men of the state he killed and to (his) father

urbem sine ulla dimicatione tradidit.
the town without any struggle he handed over
{pf}

Postea Tarquinius Superbus Ardeam urbem
Afterwards Tarquinius Superbus Ardea the town

oppugnavit. Ibi Tarquinius Collatinus sorore
attacked There Tarquinius Collatinus from a sister
{pf}

regis natus forte cenabat apud Sextum
of the king born by chance took supper at Sextus

Tarquinium	cum	aliis	iuvenibus	regiis.
Tarquinius	together with	other	young men	royal

Incidit	de			uxoribus
Occurred	about			(their) wives

It happened that they made mention of

mentio:		cum	unusquisque,
mentioning		when	each

It happened that they made mention of

suam	laudaret,	placuit	experiri.	Itaque
his own (wife)	praised	is has pleased	to do a test	Thus

equis	Romam	petunt.	Regias	nurus	in
on horses	to Rome	they went	The royal	young women	in

convivio	et	luxu	deprehendunt.	Pergant
a banquet	and	extravagance	they catch	they go

inde	Collatiam.	Lucretiam,	Collatini	uxorem,
from there	to Collatia	Lucretia	of Collatinus	the wife

inter	ancillas	in	lanificio	inveniunt.	Ea
among	(her) servants	in (while)	spinning wool	they find	She

ergo	ceteris	praestare	iudicatur.
therefore	the others	to stand above	is judged

Paucis interiectis diebus, Sextus Collatiam rediit,
A few / put in between / days / Sextus / to Collatia / returned
After a few days had passed {pf redeo}

et Lucretiae vim attulit. Illa postero die,
and / Lucretia / force / brought to / She / next / on the day
assaulted

advocatis patre et coniuge, rem
having called in / (her) father / and / (her) husband / the matter

exposuit, et se cultro, quem sub veste
revealed {pf} / and / herself / with a knife / which / under / (her) dress

texerat, occidit. Conclamant vir paterque, et
she had covered (concealed) / killed {pf} / Cry out / man / and the father / and
The husband and father cry out

in exitium regum coniurant. Tarquinio Romam
to / the demise / of the kings / they conspire / To Tarquinius / to Rome

redeunti clausae sunt urbis portae, et
returning / closed / are / of the town / the gates / and

exilium indictum.
(his) banishment / is announced

HORATIUS COCLES
Horatius / Cocles

Porsenna **rex** **Etruscorum** **ad** **restituendum**
Porsenna king of the Etruscans to reinstate

Tarquinios **cum** **infesto** **exercitu** **Romam** **venit.**
the Tarquinii with a hostile army to Rome came
{pf}

Primo **impetu** **Ianiculum** **cepit.** **Non** **usquam**
In the first onslaught the Ianiculus he took Not ever
{pf}

alias **ante** **tantus** **terror** **Romanos** **invasit.** **Ex**
at any time before so great a terror the Romans befell from
{pf}

agris **in** **urbem** **demigrant;** **urbem** **ipsam**
the countryside into the town they depart the town itself

sepiunt **praesidiis.** **Alia** **urbis** **pars**
they encircle with fortifications Another of the town part
(One)

muris, **alia** **Tiberi** **obiecto,** **tuta** **videbatur.**
by walls another by the Tiber laying in the way safe seemed

Pons **sublicius** **iter** **paene** **hostibus** **dedit,**
A bridge resting upon piles way almost to the enemies gave
(entry) (enemy) {pf}

nisi **unus** **vir** **fuisset,** **Horatius** **Cocles,**
if not one man (there) would have been Horatius Cocles

illo cognomine quod in alio proelio oculum
with that nickname because in another battle an eye
who bore that nickname

amiserat. Is pro ponte stetit, et aciem
he had lost This one in front of the bridge stood and the army
(He) {pons5} {pf}

hostium solus sustinuit, donec pons a
of the enemies alone withstood until the bridge from
{pf}

tergo interrumperetur: ipsa audacia obstupefecit
the rear was broken up by that audacity he struck dumb
{pf}

hostes; ponte rescisso, armatus in
the enemies the bridge having been cut off armed into

Tiberim desiluit, et incolumis ad suos
the Tiber he jumped down and unharmed to his own men

transnavit. Grata erga tantam virtutem civitas
swam across Grateful towards so great a courage the citizenry
(for)

fuit. Ei tantum agri datum est,
has been To him so much farmland given is
(has been)

quantum una die circumarari potuisset.
as in one day surrounded with a furrow he could
{plqmpf}

Statua quoque in comitio posita est.
A statue also in the location of the comitia placed is (was)

MUCIUS SCAEVOLA
Mucius Scaevola

Cum Porsenna Romam obsideret, Mucius vir
When Porsenna Rome besieged Mucius a man

Romanae constantiae senatum adiit, et veniam
of Roman firmness the Senate came to and permission
{pf}

transfugiendi petiit, necem regis
to flee to the other side asked the death of the king

repromittens. Accepta potestate, in castra
promising in return Being received power to the camp
(mandate)

Porsennae venit. Ibi in confertissima turba prope
of Porsenna he came There in a very dense crowd near
{pf}

regium tribunal constitit. Stipendium tunc forte
the royal court he stood still Pay then by chance
{pf}

militibus dabatur: et scriba cum
to the soldiers was (being) given and the scribe together with

rege — the king
pari — in equal
fere — almost
ornatu — attire
sedebat. — sat down
Mucius — Mucius
illum — him

pro — for
rege — the king
deceptus — being mistaken
occidit. — killed {pf}
Apprehensus — He was seized
et — and
ad — to

regem — the king
pertractus, — having been dragged
dextram — the right (hand)
accenso — kindled
ad — for

sacrificium — a sacrifice
foculo — brazier
iniecit; — he put into {pf}
hoc — that
supplicii — punishment
a — from

rea — the guilty (hand)
exigens, — exacting
quod — which
in — in
caede — the killing
peccasset. — had sinned (made a mistake)

Attonitus — Taken aback
miraculo — by (this) marvellous deed
rex — the king
iuvenem — the young man

amoveri — to be moved away
ab — from
altaribus — the altars
iussit. — ordered {pf}
Tum — Then
Mucius, — Mucius

quasi — as if
beneficium — a favour
remunerans, — remunerating
ait — says
trecentos, — (that) three hundred

sui — to himself
similes, — similar
adversus — against
eum — him
coniurasse. — have conspired
Qua — By which

re   ille,   territus, bellum,   acceptis   obsidibus,
thing   he   frightened the war having received   hostages
(event) (the king)

deposuit.
put down
(gave up)

CLOELIA VIRGO
Cloelia   the maiden

Porsenna   Cloeliam   virginem   nobilem   inter
Porsenna   Cloelia   a maiden   noble   among

obsides accepit. Cum eius castra haud procul
the hostages received Because his camp not far
    {pf}

ripa   Tiberis   locata   essent,   Cloelia
from the bank of the Tiber located was Cloelia

deceptis   custodibus noctu egressa, equum,
having been eluded the guards at night gone out a horse

quem sors dederat, arripuit, et Tiberim traiecit.
which fortune had given seized and the Tiber crossed
    {pf}

Quod ubi regi nuntiatum est, primo ille,
What where to the king reported is first he
(That) (when)   (has been)

incensus ira, Romam legatos misit ad Cloeliam
roused by anger to Rome envoys sent to Cloelia
{pf}

obsidem reposcendam. Romani eam ex
the hostage claim back The Romans her out of
{grv} (according to)

foedere restituerunt. Tum rex virginis
the treaty gave back Then the king of the maiden

virtutem admiratus, eam laudavit, ac parte
the courage having admired her praised and part
{pf}

obsidum donare se dixit, permisitque
of the hostages to give as a present he he said and he permitted
{pf} {pf}

ut ipsa quos vellet, legeret. Productis
that she whom she willed would choose Having been brought up

obsidibus, Cloelia virgines puerosque elegit, quorum
the hostages Cloelia girls and boys chose whose

aetatem iniuriae obnoxiam sciebat, et cum
age to injury liable she knew and together with

eis in patriam rediit. Romani novam in
them to the home town she returned The Romans new in
{pf}

femina virtutem novo genere honoris, statua
a woman (her) courage with a new kind of honour a statue

equestri, donavere. In summa via sacra,
equestrian have rewarded At the highest point of the Via Sacra

fuit posita virgo insidens equo.
has been placed a maiden sitting on a horse

Chapter V

MENENII AGRIPPAE FABULA
Of Menenius / Agrippa / a Fable

Menenius — Menenius
Agrippa — Agrippa
concordiam — harmony
inter — between
patres — the Fathers

plebemque — and the common people
restituit. — restored {pf}
Nam — For
cum — when

plebs — the common people
a — from
patribus — the Fathers
secessisset, — seceded
quod — because

tributum — tax
et — and
militiam — military service
non — not
toleraret, — it (could) bear
Agrippa — Agrippa

vir — a man
facundus, — eloquent
ad — to
plebem — the common people
missus est; — is sent (was)
qui — who

intromissus — having been admitted
in — into
castra — the camp
nihil — nothing
aliud — other (else)
quam — than

narrasse fertur: "Olim humani artus,
to have told a story / is brought (told) / Once upon a time / the human / limbs

cum ventrem otiosum cernerent, ab eo
when / the belly (stomach) / idle / they perceived / from / it (with)

discordaverunt, conspiraveruntque ne manus
were at variance {pf} / and they plotted {pf} / that neither / the hands

ad os cibum ferrent, nec os acciperet
to the / mouth / food / would bring / nor / the mouth / would accept

datum, nec dentes conficerent. At dum
what was given / nor / the teeth / chop (it) / But / while

ventrem domare volunt, ipsi quoque
the belly / to tame / they want / they themselves / also

defecerunt, totumque corpus ad extremam tabem
grew weak {pf} / and the whole / body / to / extreme / decay

venit: inde apparuit ventris haud segne
came {pf} / therefrom / it became visible {pf} / of the belly / not / a lazy

ministerium esse, eumque acceptos cibos
office / to be / and it / the received / food {cibus4pl}
and that it distributed

44

per omnia membra disserere, et cum eo in
by all limbs to distribute and with it to
(among) and that it distributed

gratiam redierunt. Sic senatus et populus
(good) grace came back So the Senate and the common people

quasi unum corpus discordia pereunt, concordia
as if one body by discord perish by concord
(like)

valent."
are strong

Hac fabula, Menenius flexit hominum mentes.
By this fable Menenius bent of people the minds
{pf}

Plebs in urbem regressa est. Creavit
the common people to the town come back is It created
(has) {pf}

tamen tribunos, qui libertatem suam adversus
however tribunes who liberty its against

nobilitatis superbiam defenderent. Paulo post
of the nobility the haughtiness would defend A litlle after

mortuus est Menenius, vir omni vita pariter
died is Menenius a man in (his) whole life equally
(has)

patribus ac plebi carus;
to the Fathers and the common people dear

post restitutam civium
after the restored of the citizens
after the restoration of the harmony

concordiam carior plebi
concord more dear to the common people
after the restoration of the harmony

factus. Is tamen in tanta paupertate decessit,
he has become He however to so great poverty lapsed
{pf}

ut eum populus collatis quadrantibus
that him the common people collected farthings
after collecting farthings

sepeliret, locum sepulcro senatus publice
buried a place for the grave the Senate at public expense

daret. Potest consolari pauperes Menenius, sed
gave Was able to comfort the poor Menenius but

multo magis docere locupletes, quam solidam
much more to teach the wealthy how solid
(real)

laudem cupienti non sit necessaria nimis
praise for him who desires not is necessary too
(glory) {coni}

anxia divitiarum comparatio.
(eager / of riches / acquisition)

QUINCTIUS CINCINNATUS
(Quinctius / Cincinnatus)

Aequi consulem Minucium atque exercitum eius
(The Aequi / the consul / Minucius / and / army / his)

circumcessos tenebant: id ubi Romae nuntiatum
(surrounded / held / this / where (when) / at Rome / reported)

est, tantus pavor, tanta trepidatio fuit, quanta
(is (was) / so much / fear / so much / consternation / there was {pf} / as much)

si urbem ipsam, non castra, hostes obsiderent:
(as if / the town / itself / not / the camp / the enemies / besieged)

cum autem in altero consule parum esse
(when / however / in / the other / consul / little / to be)

praesidii videretur, dictatorem dici
(help / was seen / a dictator / to be appointed)

placuit, qui rem afflictam restitueret.
(is has pleased / who / the thing (situation) / shattered / would restore)

Quinctius Cincinnatus, omnium consensu, dictator
Quinctius Cincinnatus of all by consensus dictator

est dictus. Ille spes unica imperii Romani
is appointed That one hope only of the empire Roman
(was) (He)

trans Tiberim quatuor iugerum colebat
on the other side the Tiber four acres cultivated

agrum. Ad quem missi legati nudum eum
farmland To him sent the envoys naked him
The to him sent envoys

arantem offenderint. Salute data invicem
plowing came upon Greeting having been given reciprocally

redditaque, Quinctius togam propere e tugurio
and given back Quinctius (his) toga in haste from (his) cottage

proferre uxorem Raciliam iussit, ut
to bring forth (his) wife Racilia ordered in order that
{pf}

senatus mandata togatus audiret.
of the Senate the orders dessed in toga he would hear

Postquam absterso pulvere ac sudore, toga
After wiped off the dust and the sweat the toga
{pp abstergo}

indutus **processit** **Quinctius,** **dictatorem** **eum**
having been put on came out Quinctius the dictator him

legati **gratulantes** **consalutant,** **quantus** **terror**
the envoys congratulating greeted (and) how much terror

in **exercitu** **sit** **exponunt.** **Quinctius** **igitur**
in the army there is expounded Quinctius So
(was)

Romam **venit,** **et** **antecedentibus** **lictoribus** **domum**
to Rome came and preceding (him) lictores home
{pf}

deductus est. **Postero** **die** **profectus,** **caesis**
conducted is On the next day having left having cut down
has been conducted

hostibus, **exercitum** **Romanum** **liberavit.** **Urbem**
the enemies the army Roman he delivered The town

triumphant **ingressus** **est.** **Duces** **hostium**
triumphing entered he is The leaders of the enemies
(has)

ante **currum** **ducti,** **militaria** **signia**
in front of (his) chariot (were) led military standards

praelata: **secutus** **est** **exercitus** **praeda**
(were) carried in front followed is the army with booty
(has)

onustus;   epulae   instructae   ante   omnium
laden   dishes of food   (were) provided   in front of   of all

domos.   Quinctius   sexto   decimo   die
the houses   Quinctius   on the sixth   tenth   day
   (-teenth)

dictatura,   quam   in   sex   menses   acceperat,
from the dictatorship   which   for   six   months   he had received

se   abdicavit,   et   ad   boves   rediit   triumphalis
himself   resigned   and   to   the oxen   went back   (as) a triumphant
   {pf}

agricola.
peasant

CAIUS MARCIUS CORIOLANUS
Caius   Marcius   Coriolanus

Caius   Marcius   gentis   patriciae,   a   captis
Caius   Martius   of a tribe   patrician   from   conquered (by him)

Coriolis   urbe   Volscorum   Coriolanus   dictus est.
Corioli   a town   of the Volsci   Coriolanus   named   is
   got his name

Patre   orbatus   adhuc   puer   sub   matris
Of (his) father   bereft   still   a boy   under   of (his) mother

tutela **adolevit.** **Sortitus** **erat** **a** **natura**
the tutelage | he grew up {pf} | Obtained | he was (had) | from | nature

nobiles **ad** **laudem** **impetus.** **Sed** **quia** **doctrina** **non**
noble | to (for) | praise (glory) | fervour | but | as | instruction | not

accessit, **irae** **impotens,** **obstinataeque**
had come with it | over (his) anger | powerless (without control) | and of an obstinate

pervicaciae **fuit.** **Cum** **prima** **stipendia** **facere**
stubbornness | he was {pf} | When | first | military service | to do

coepisset **adolescens,** **e** **multis** **proeliis** **quibus**
he had begun | as a youth | from | the many | battles | at which

interfuit **nunquam** **rediit,** **nisi** **donatus**
he was present {pf} | never | he returned {pf} | if not | presented

coroni **aliove** **militari** **praemio.** **In** **omni**
with a garland | or another | military | prize | In | every

vitae **ratione** **nihil** **aliud** **sibi** **proponebat**
of (his) life | consideration | nothing | else | to himself | he proposed

quam **ut** **matri** **placeret:** **cumque** **illa**
than | that | to (his) mother | he would please | and when | she

audiret **filium** **laudari,** **aut** **corona** **donari**
heard — (her) son — to be praised — or — a garland — to be given

videret, **tum** **demum** **felicem** **se** **putabat.**
saw — then — only — happy — herself — she considered

Ea **oblectanda** **et** **colenda** **satiari** **non**
(of) her — to please — and — to venerate — get enough — not
of pleasing and venerating her

poterat. **Illa** **cupiente,** **uxorem** **duxit:** **illius** **in**
could — She — wishing — a wife — he led — of her — in
         On her wish —   (he took)

aedibus **cum** **uxore** **habitavit.**
house — with — (his) wife — he dwelled
            {pf}

Coriolanum, **post** **victoriam** **eius** **opera** **maxime**
Coriolanus — after — the victory — by his — effort — mostly
                       {opera5}

partam, **Posthumius** **consul** **apud**
obtained — Posthumius — The consul — in the presence of
{ptps pario}

milites **laudavit:** **eum** **militaribus** **donis** **onerare**
the soldiers — praised — him — with military — gifts — to load
        {pf}

voluit; **agri** **centum** **iugera,** **decem** **captivos,**
he wanted — of farmland — one hundred — acres — ten — captives
{pf}

totidem	ornatos	equos,	centum	boves	et
as many	equipped	horses	one hundred	heads of cattle	and

argenti	pondus	quantum	sustinere	potuisset,
of silver	a weight	as big	hold up (carry)	(as) he could {pf}

offerebat.	Coriolanus	vero	nihil	ex	his
he offered	Coriolanus	however	nothing	out of	these

omnibus	accepit,	praeter	unius	hospitis	captivi
all	accepted {pf}	other than	of one	guest-friend {hospes2}	captive

salutem	et	equum.	Consul	factus,
the safety	and	the horse	(He,) consul	having been made

gravi	annona	advectum	e	Sicilia
in a heavy	grain year	imported	from	Sicilia
the grain price that year being high				

frumentum	magno	pretio,	dandum	populo
(that) corn	at a great (at a high)	price	for being given	to the people

curavit,	ut	plebs	agros,	non
he saw to it	in order that	the common people	the fields	not

seditiones	coleret.	Qua	de	causa
insurrections	would cultivate	Which	from	cause

damnatus — having been condemned
ad — to
Volscos — the Volsci
concessit, — he went off
eosque — and them

adversus — against
Romanos — the Romans
concitavit. — roused {pf}
Imperator — Military commander
a — by

Volscis — the Volsci
factus, — having been made
ad — at
quartum — the fourth
ab — from
urbe — the town

lapidem — (mile)stone
castra — camp
posuit, — he pitched
et — and
agrum — the farmland
Romanum — Roman

est — he is (he has)
populatus. — ravaged

Missi — Sent
sunt — are (were)
Roma — from Rome {Roma5}
ad — to
Coriolanum — Coriolanus
oratores — envoys

de — concerning
pace, — peace
sed — but
atrox — a fierce
responsum — answer
retulerunt. — they brought back {pf}

Iterum — a second time
deinde — thereupon
missi, — sent
ne — not
in — into
castra — the army camp

quidem — even
recepti — received
sunt. — they are (were)
Sacerdotes — The priests
quoque — also
suis — in their

infulis **velati** **ad** **eum** **iverunt** **supplices,**
sacred headbands   wrapped   to   him   went   (as) supplicants

nec **magis** **animum** **eius** **flexerunt:** **stupebat**
and not   more   mind   his   bent {pf}   was benumbed

senatus, **trepidabat** **populus,** **viri** **pariter** **ac**
the Senate   trembled   the people   men   equally   and

mulieres **exitium** **imminens** **lamentabantur.** **Tum**
women   the death   imminent   bewailed   Then

Veturia, **Coriolani** **mater,** **et** **Volumnia** **uxor**
Veturia   Coriolanus'   mother   and   Volumnia   (his) wife

duos **parvos** **filios** **secum** **trahens,** **castra**
(his) two   little   sons   with herself   taking along   the camp

hostium **petierunt.** **Ubi** **matrem** **aspexit**
of the enemies   went to   Where (When)   (his) mother   he beheld {pf}

Coriolanus: **"O** **patria** **inquit,** **vicisti** **iram**
Coriolanus   O   fatherland   he said   you have defeated (overcome)   wrath

meam **admotis** **matris** **meae** **precibus,**
my   by the brought forward   of mother   my   pleas

55

cui tuam in me iniuriam condono."
to whom your towards me injury I forgive

Complexus inde suos castra movit, et
Having embraced thereupon his people the camp he moved and
{pf}

exercitum ex agro Romano abduxit.
the army from the territory Roman led away

Coriolanus postea a Volscis, ut proditor, occisus
Coriolanus afterwards by the Volsci as a traitor was killed

dicitur.
it is said

Chapter VI

MARCUS **FURIUS** **CAMILLUS.** **ROMA** **A** **GALLIS**
Marcus Furius Calimmus Rome by the Gauls

INVASA
invaded

Cum **Marcus** **Furius** **Camillus** **urbem** **Falerios**
When Marcus Furius Camillos the town Falirii

obsideret, **ludi** **magister** **plurimos** **et**
besieged of the play the master several and
(of the school)

nobilissimos **inde** **pueros,** **velut**
most noble from there boys as if

ambulandi **gratia,** **eductos,** **in**
to take a stroll grace having been led out into
with the purpose of taking a stroll

castra **Romanorum** **perduxit:** **quibus** **Camillo**
the army camp of the Romans brought who to Camillus
{pf}

traditis, **non erat dubium quin**
having been delivered / not / (there) was / doubt / but that

Falisci, deposito bello, sese
the Falerians / having been given up / war / themselves

Romanis dedituri essent; sed Camillus
to the Romans / about to surrender / would be / but / Camillus

perfidiam proditoris detestatus: "Non ad similem
the perfidy / of the traitor / (having) detested / Not / to / one like

tui inquit, venisti; sunt belli sicut et
you {tuus2} / he said / you have come / (there) are / of war / just as / also

pacis iura: arma habemus non adversus eam
of peace / laws / arms / we have / not / against / that

aetatem cui etiam captis urbibus parcitur,
age / which {quis3} / also / having been taken / after the reduction of towns / the towns / is spared

sed adversus armatos qui castra Romana
but / against / armed men / who / the camp / Roman

oppugnaverunt." Denudari deinde ludi
have assailed / to be denuded (To be undressed) / thereupon / the school

magistrum   iussit   eum   in   urbem   reducendum
master   he ordered   him   to   the town   to bring back
{pf}

pueris   tradidit,   manibus   post   tergum   alligatis,
to the boys   he gave over   the hands   behind   (his) back   bound
{pf}

virgasque   eis   dedit,   quibus   euntem
and sticks   to them   he gave   with which   him going
{pf}

verberarent.   Statim   Falisci,   beneficio   magis
they should beat   At once   the Falerians   by the benefaction   more

quam   armis   victi,   portas   Romanis   aperuerunt.
than   by arms   defeated   the gates   to the Romans   opened
{pf}

Camillus   post   multa   in   patriam   merita
Camillus   after   many   towards   the fatherland   merits

iudicio   populi   damnatus   exsulatum   abiit.
by the sentence   of the people   condemned   into exile   went away
{pf}

Urbe   egrediens   ab   Diis   precatus   esse
From the town   going out   from   the gods   prayed   to be
(to have)

dicitur,   ut   si   innoxio   sibi   ea   iniuria
he is said   that   if   innocent   to himself   that   injury

fieret,	desiderium	sui	facerent
had been done	wish	his	they would do
			(they would carry out)

ingratae	patriae	quamprimum:	neque	multo
to the ungrateful	fatherland	as soon as possible	and not	much

postea	res	evenit.	Nam	Galli	Senones
later	the thing	came to pass	For	the Gauls	Senonian
	(the issue)				

Clusium,	Etruriae	oppidum,	obsederunt.
Clusium	of Etruria	a fortified town	besieged
			{pf obsideo}

Clusini	novo	bello	exterriti	ab
The men of Clusium	by the new	war	terrified	from
	(by the sudden)			

Romanis	auxilium	petierunt.	Missi	sunt	Roma
the Romans	help	asked	Sent	are	from Rome
		{pf}		(were)	

tres	legati,	qui	Gallos	monerent	ut	ab
three	envoys	who	the Gauls	warned	that	from

oppugnatione	desisterent.	Ex	his	legatis	unus
the siege	they would desist	out of	these	envoys	one

contra	ius	gentium	in	aciem	processit,	et
against	the law	of nations	into	the battle	went forth	and
	international law					

ducem **Senonum** **interfecit.** **Qua** **re** **commoti**
the .leader | of the Senones | killed {pf} | By which | thing (event) | excited

Galli, **petitis** **in** **deditionem** **legatis** **nec**
the Gauls | having required | to | surrender | the envoys | and not

impetratis, **ad** **urbem** **venerunt** **et** **exercitum**
obtaining | to | the town (Rome) | came {pf} | and | the army

Romanum **apud** **Alliam** **fluvium** **ceciderunt** **die**
Roman | near | Allia | the river | slaughtered {pf caedo} | on the day

decimo **sexto** **calendas** **Augusti:** **qui** **dies,**
tenth | sixth | after the first day | of August | which | day

inter **nefastos** **relatus,** **Alliensis** **dictus** **est.**
among | the unlucky (days) | remembered | Allia-day | named | is

Galli **victores** **paulo** **ante** **solis** **occasum** **ad**
The Gauls | victors (victiorious) | by little (not long) | before | of the sun | setting sunset | at

urbem **Romam** **perveniunt.** **Postquam** **hostes**
the town | Rome | arrived {pf} | After | the enemies

adesse **nuntiatum** **est,** **iuventus** **Romana**
to be there | reported | is (were) | the youth | Roman

duce — by the leader / with M as leader
Manlio — Manlius
in — into
arcem — the citadel
conscendit; — ascended {pf}

seniores — the elder people
vero — however
domos — (their) houses
ingressi — having entered

adventum — the coming
Gallorum — of the Gauls
obstinato — resolved
ad — to
mortem — death
animo — with a mind

expectabant. — awaited
Qui — (Those) who
inter — among
eos — them
curules — curulian

magistratus — offices
gesserant, — had borne (held)
ornati — adorned
honorum — of honours
insignibus — with the signs / with their honorific signs

in — in
vestibulis — the entrances
aedium — of (their) houses
eburneis — on ivory
sellis — seats
insederunt — sat down {pf insido}

ut — in order that
cum — when
venisset — would come
hostis, — the enemy
in — in
sua — their
dignitate — dignity

morerentur. — they would die
Interim — In the meantime
Galli — the Gauls
domos — the houses
patentes — open

ingressi — having gone into
vident — see (saw)
viros — men
ornatu — by apparel
et — and
vultus — of face

maiestate Diis simillimos: cum Galli ad
majesty | to the gods | most similar | when | the Gauls | towards

eos veluti simulacra, conversi starent, unus ex
them | as if | statues | turned | stood | one | out of

his senibus dicitur Gallo barbam suam
these | old men | is said | to a Gaul | beard | his

permulcenti scipionem eburneum in caput
gently touching | staff | ivory | on | the head

incussisse. Iratus Gallus eum occidit: ab eo
to have struck | Angered | the Gaul | him | killed {pf} | from | that

initium caedis ortum est. Deinde ceteri
the beginning | of the slaughter | started | is (has) | Thereupon | others

omnes in sedibus suis trucidati sunt.
all | in (on) | chairs | their | massacred | are (were)

Galli deinde impetum facere in arcem
The Gauls | thereupon | an attack | to make | to | the citadel

statuunt. Primo, militem qui tentaret viam
decided {pf} | First | a soldier | that he {ut is} | would attempt | the way

praemiserunt. Tum nocte sublustri sublevantes
they sent ahead Then in a night half-dark supporting
{pf}

invicem et trahentes alii alios in summum
each other and dragging the ones the others to the highest
one another

saxum evaserunt, tanto silentio ut non solum
rock they came up such in silence that not only
{pf}

custodes fallerent, sed ne canes quidem,
the guards they deceived but not the dogs even

sollicitum animal, excitarent. Anseres autem non
watchful animal they awoke The geese however not

fefellerunt, quibus in summa inopia Romani
they deceived from whom in the highest scarcity the Romans

abstinuerant, quia aves erant Iunoni sacrae;
had abstained because birds they were to Iuno sacred

quae res Romanis saluti fuit. Namque
which thing for the Romans to salvation was For
{pf}

clangore anserum alarumque crepitu
by the noise of the geese and of (their) wings by the rustling

excitus, Manlius vir bello egregius, ceteros ad
awoken — Manlius — a man — in war — outstanding — the others — to

arma vocans Gallos ascendentes deiecit:
arms — calling — the Gauls — climbing up — threw down {pf}

unde mos iste incessit ut solemni pompa,
from where — custom — that — has come — that — in a solemn — procession

canis in furca suffixus feratur; anser vero
a dog — at — a forked branch — attached — was carried — a goose — but

velut triumphans in lectica et veste stragula
as if — in triumph — in — a litter — and — on a cloth — spread out

gestetur.
was carried

Tunc consensu omnium placuit ab exilio
Then — with the consent — of all — it has pleased — from — exile

Camillum acciri; missi igitur ad eum legati
Camillus — to be called — (were) sent — therefore — to — him — envoys

ipseque dictator absens dictus est. Interim
and he — dictator — absent — appointed — is (was) — In the meantime

fames	utrumque	exercitum	urgebat:	at,	ne
hunger	each	army	beset	but	that not

Galli	putarent	Romanos	ea	necessitate	ad
the Gauls	would believe	the Romans	by	that need	to

deditionem	cogi,	multis	locis	de
surrender	to be compelled	in	many places	from

Capitolio	panis	iactatus	est	in	hostium	stationes.
the Capirol	bread	thrown	is (was)	to	of the enemies	outposts

Ea	re	adducti	sunt	Galli	ut	haud
By that	thing	induced	are (were)	the Gaulus	that	with a not

magna	mercede	obsidionem	relinquerent.	Pactum
large	compensation	the siege	they would leave (lift)	agreed {pf paciscor}

est	pretium	mille	pondo	auri.	Nondum
is (there was)	a price	a thousand	pound(s)	of gold	Not yet

omni	auro	appenso	Camillus	dictator	intervenit,
all	gold	hanged (weighed out)	Camillus	dictator	intervened

collectis	Romani	exercitus	reliquiis.
having been gathered	of the Roman	army	the remains

Auferri aurum de medio iubet,
to be carried away the gold from the middle he ordered

denuntiatque Gallis ut se ad proelium
he let know to the Gauls that they for battle

expediant. Instruit deinde aciem, et
would make ready he drew up thereupon the battle order and

Gallos internecione occidit. Ne nuntius
the Gauls in a wholesale slaughter cut down Not a messenger

quidem cladis relictus est. Dictator, recuperata
even of the defeat left over is The dictator being regained
(was)

ex hostibus patria, triumphans urbem
from the enemies the fatherland triumphing the town

ingressus est, et a militibus parens patriae,
entered is and by the soldiers father of the fatherland
has

conditorque alter urbis appellatus est.
founder another of the town named is
(a second) (was)

Chapter VII

TITUS MANLIUS TORQUATUS
Titus　　Manlius　　Torquatus

Titus Manlius ob ingenii et linguae
Titus　Manlius　because　of his intelligence　and　tongue

tarditatem a patre rus relegatus
the slowness　by　(his) father　to the countryside　sent away

fuerat. Cum audisset patri diem dictam esse
had been　When　he had heard　to his father　a day　told　to be
　　　　　　　　　　　that his father had been suppoenaed

a Pomponio tribuno plebis, cepit consilium
by　Pomponius　tribune　of the plebs　he took　a plan

rudis quidem et agrestis animi, sed pietate
rude　to be sure　and　of a rustic　mind　but　for its piety
(clumsy)　　　　　(of a coarse)

laudabile. Cultro succinctus mane in
praiseworthy　With a knife　in his belt　early in the morning　to

urbem, atque a porta confestim ad Pomponium
the town and from the gate straight to Pomponius

pergit: introductus cultrum stringit, et super
he goes having been let in the knife he pulls and over

lectum Pomponii stans, se eum transfixurum
the bed Pomponius' standing (that) he him is going to transfix

minatur nisi ab incoepta accusatione desistat.
he threatens if not from the started indictment he desists

Pavidus tribunus, quippe qui cerneret ferrum ante
Trembling the tribune because who saw the iron before
as he

oculos micare, accusationem demisit. Ea res
(his) eyes gleam the indictment let go This thing
{pf} (deed)

adolescenti honori fuit, quod animum eius
to the young man to honour was because mind his
{pf}

acerbitas paterna a pietate non avertisset,
the sternness fatherly from piety not had turned away

ideoque eodem anno tribunus militum factus
and therefore iin the same year tribune of the army made

est.
he is
(he was)

Cum postea Galli ad tertium lapidem trans
When afterwards the Gauls at the third (mile)stone across

Anionem fluvium castra posuissent, exercitus
Anio the river (their) camp had pitched the army

Romanus ab urbe profectus est, et in citeriore
Roman from the town departed is and on this side
(has)

ripa fluvii constitit. Pons in medio
on the bank of the river took its stand A bridge in the middle
{pf}

erat: tunc Gallus eximia corporis
was then a Gaul with an extraordinary of the body

magnitudine in vacuum pontem processit, et
size to the empty bridge went forth and

quam maxima voce potuit: "Quem nunc,"
which greatest with a voice he could Whom now
as loud as he could

inquit, "Roma fortissimum habet, is procedat ad
he said Rome the most strong has he let come forth to

pugnam, a fight   **ut** in order that   **eventus** the outcome   **ostendat** shows   **utra** which of both

gens people   **bello** in war   **sit** be (is)   **melior."** better   **Diu** A long time   **inter** among   **primores** the foremost

iuvenum of the young men   **Romanorum** Roman   **silentium** silence   **fuit.** (there) was   **Tum** Then

Titus Titus   **Manlius** Manlius   **ex** from   **statione** (his) station   **ad** to   **imperatorem** the army commander

pergit: goes   **"Iniussu** Unbidden   **tuo,"** your (by you)   **inquit,** he says   **"imperator,** commander   **extra** outside

ordinem the battle order   **nunquam** never   **pugnaverim,** I have fought   **non,** not (even)   **si** if

certam certain   **victoriam** a victory   **videam.** I saw   **Si** If   **tu** you   **permittis,** permit (it)   **volo** I want

isti to that   **belluae** beast   **ostendere** show   **me** I {ego4}   **ex** from   **ea** that   **familia** family   **ortum** born

esse, to be   **quae** which   **Gallorum** of Gauls   **agmen** the band   **ex** from   **rupe** the rock   **Tarpeia** Tarpeian

deturbavit. **Cui** **imperator:** **"Macte**
has dislodged To whom the commander Lucky

virtute," **inquit,** **"Tite** **Manli,** **esto:** **perge,** **et**
with your courage he said o Titus Manlius be go and

nomen **Romanum** **invictum** **praesta."**
the name Roman (is) unvincible show (that)

Armant **deinde** **iuvenem** **aequales:** **scutum** **capit,**
Arm thereupon the youth his peers a shield he takes
His peer's arm the youth

Hispano **cingitur** **gladio** **ad** **propiorem** **pugnam**
with a Spanish he is girded sword for more nearby fight

habili. **Expectabat** **eum** **Gallus** **solide** **laetus** **et**
appropriate Awaited him the Gaul wholly glad and

linguam **ab** **irrisu** **exserens.** **Ubi**
(his) tongue from mocking sticking out Where
mockingly (when)

constiterunt **inter** **duas** **acies,** **Gallus**
they had taken their stand between the two lines of battle the Gaul

ensem **cum** **ingenti** **sonitu** **in** **arma** **Manlii**
(his) sword with a great sound on the arms of Manlius

deiecit. **Manlius** **vero** **insinuavit** **sese** **inter**
brought down / Manlius / however / insinuated / himself / between
{pf} {pf}

corpus **et** **arma** **Galli,** **atque** **uno** **et**
the body / and / the weapon / of the Gaul; / and / with one / and

altero **ictu** **ventrem** **transfodit.** **Iacenti**
another / blow / the belly / pierced / To (him) laying down
{pf}

torquem **detraxit,** **quem** **cruore** **respersum** **collo**
(his) necklace / he tore off / which / with blood / sprinkled / neck
{pf}

circumdedit **suo.** **Defixerat** **pavor** **cum**
he put around / his / Struck dumb / fear / (mixed) with
{pf} {pf}

admiratione **Gallos;** **Romani** **alacres** **obviam** **militi**
admiration / the Gauls / The Romans / cheerful / towards / soldier

suo **progrediuntur,** **et** **gratulantes** **laudantesque** **ad**
their / advance / and / congratulating / and praising (him) / to

imperatorem **perducunt.** **Manlius** **inde** **Torquati**
the commander / conduct / Manlius / from that / of Torquatus

nomen **accepit.**
the name / has received

Idem **Manlius,** **postea** **consul** **factus,** **bello**
The same | Manlius | later | consul | appointed | in the war

Latino **ut** **disciplinam** **militarem**
Latin (with the Latins) | in order that | discipline | military

restitueret, **edixit** **ne** **quis** **extra**
he would restore | has proclaimed | that not | anybody | outside

ordinem **in** **hostes** **pugnaret.** **Forte**
the battle order | to | the enemies | should give battle | By chance

filius **eius** **accessit** **prope** **stationem** **hostium:**
son | his | came to {pf} | near | a post | of the enemies

is **qui** **Latino** **equitatui** **praeerat** **ubi**
he (the soldier) | who | the Latin | cavalry | commanded | where (when)

consulis **filium** **agnovit,** **"Visne,"** **inquit,**
of the consul | the son | recognized {pf agnosco} | Don't you want | he said

"congredi **mecum** **ut** **singularis** **proelii**
join battle | with me | that | of a single | fight

eventu **cernatur** **quantam** **eques** **Latinus**
from the outcome | may be seen | how much | a horseman | Latin

Romano	praestet?"	Movit	ferocem	animum
the Roman	is superior to	Stirred {pf}	the fierce	mind

iuvenis	seu	ira,	seu	detractandi	certaminis
of the youth	be it	anger	be it	of ducking	a battle

pudor.	Oblitus	itaque	imperii	paterni	in
shame	Forgetful	so	of the command	fatherly	into

certamen	ruit,	et	Latinum	ex	equo
the engagement	he rushes {pf}	and	the Latin	off	(his) horse

excussum	transfixit,	spoliisque	lectis
having thrown	pierced him {pf transfigo}	and the spoils	having been picked up after picking up the booty

in	castra	ad	patrem	venit.	Extemplo	filium
into	the camp	to	his father	he came {pf}	Straightaway	(his) son

aversatus	consul	milites	classico
having been turned away	the consul	the soldiers	by a trumpet call

advocat:	qui	postquam	frequentes	convenerunt:
calls together	who	thereafter	in great numbers	came together {pf}

"Quandoquidem"	inquit,	"tu,	fili,	contra	imperium
Since	he said	you	son	against	the command

consulis — of the consul
pugnasti — have battled
oportet — it is becoming
ut — that
disciplinam — discipline

poena — by judgment
tua — your
restituas. — you restore
Triste — Sad
exemplum, — an example
sed — but
in — to (for)

posterum — the future
salubre — salutary
iuventuti — to the youth
eris. — you will be
"I, — Go,
lictor, — lictor

deliga — bind (him)
ad — to
palum." — the execution stake
Metu — By fear
omnes — all

obstupuerunt; — were stupefied {pf}
sed — but
postquam — after
cervice — the neck
caesa — having been cut

when the neck had been cut

fusus — flown
est — is (has)
cruor, — the blood
in — into
questus — complaints
et — and
lamenta — laments

eruperunt. — they burst {pf erumpo}
Manlio — To Manlius
Romam — to Rome
redeunti — returning
seniores — the elder people

tantum — only
obviam — to meet
exierunt: — came out {pf}
iuventus — the young people
et — and
tunc — then

eum — him
et — and
omni — whole
deinde — thereafter
vita — (during his) life
exsecrata — cursed
est. — is (has)

PUBLIUS DECIUS MUS
Publius   Decius   Mus

Decius   sub   Valerio   consule   tribunus   militum
Decius   under   Valerius   consul   tribune   of the military

fuit.   Cum   exercitus   Romanus   in   angustiis   clausus
was   When   the army   Roman   in   a defile   closed in
{pf esse}

esset,   Decius   conspexit   editum   collem
was   Decius   noticed   an elevated   hill
{pf conspicio}

imminentem   hostium   castris.   Accepto
overlooking   of the enemies   the camp   Having received

praesidio   verticem   occupavit,   hostes   terruit,
reinforcement   the top   he occupied   the enemies   he terrified
{pf}   {pf}

et   spatium   consuli   dedit   ad   subducendum
and   space   to the consul   he gave   for   leading away
{pf}

agmen   in   aequiorem   locum.   Ipse
the army column   to   a more level   place   He himself

intempesta   nocte   per   medias   hostium
in a dark   night   through   (the) middle   of the enemies

custodias — the guardposts
somno — by sleep
oppressas — having been overcome
incolumis — unharmed

evasit. — escaped {pf evado}
Quare — For which
ab — by
exercitu — the army
donatus — been given
est — he is (he has)

corona civica, — a garland citizen / a civic recognition
quae — which
dabatur — is given
ei — to him
qui — who
obsidione — from investment

cives — the citizens
liberasset. — had liberated
Consul — Consul
fuit — he has been
bello — in the war
Latino — Latin

cum — together with
Manlio — Manlius
Torquato. — Torquatus
Tunc — Then
utrique — to each of both

consuli — consul(s)
somnio — in a dream
obvenisset — came (that)
eum — that {is4}
populum — people
victorem — victor(ious)

fore, — was to be
cuius — whose
dux — leader
in — in
proelio — the battle
cecidisset. — would have fallen

Convenit — iI (was) agreed
inter — between
eos, — them
ut — that
is — he
cuius — whose
cornu — (army) wing
in — in

acie — the battle order
laboraret, — would get into trouble
Diis — to the gods / divine ghosts of the dead

se   Manibus   devoveret.   Inclinante   sua
himself   of the netherworld   would vow   When gave way   his
        divine ghosts of the dead

parte,   Decius   se   et   hostes   Diis
part (of the army)   Decius   himself   and   the enemies   to the gods

Manibus   devovit.   Armatus   in   equum
of the netherworld   vowed   Fully armed   on   (his) horse
           {pf}

insiluit,   ac   se   in   medios   hostes   immisit.
he jumped   and   himself   into   the midst   (of) the enemies   charged
                      {hostis4}

Corruit   obrutus   telis,   et   victoriam
He fell down   overwhelmed   ·   by spears   and   the victory
{pf}

suis   reliquit.
for his people   left behind

SPURIUS POSTHUMIUS ET CLADES AD FURCULAS
Spurius   Posthumius   and   the defeat   at   the Forks

CAUDINAS
Caudine

Spurius   Posthumius   consul   cum   bellum   adversus
Spurius   Posthumus   consul   when   war   against

Samnites **gereret,** **a** **Pontio** **Telesino** **duce**
the Samnites he borne by Pontius from Telesa leader
(he waged)

hostium **in** **insidias** **inductus** **est:** **is** **namque**
of the enemies into an ambush led is he for
(was)

simulatos **transfugas** **misit** **qui** **Romanos** **monerent**
would-be deserters sent who the Romans warned
{pf}

Luceriam, **Apuliae** **urbem,** **a** **Samnitibus** **obsideri.**
Luceria of Apulia a town by the Samnites to be besieged

Non **erat** **dubium** **quin** **Romani**
Not it was in doubt that not the Romans
(that)

Lucerinis, **bonis** **ac** **fidelibus** **sociis,** **opem**
to the people of Luceria good and faithful allies help

ferrent. **Luceriam** **duae** **viae** **ducebant,** **altera**
would bring To Luceria two roads led the other
(one)

longior **et** **tutior,** **altera** **brevior** **et** **periculosior.**
longer and safer the other shorter and more dangerous

Festinatio **breviorem** **elegit.** **Itaque** **cum** **in**
Speed the shorter one chose Therefore when into
{pf}

insidias **venissent,** **qui** **locus** **Furculae** **Caudinae**
an ambush · they had come · which · place · The Forks · Caudine

vocabatur, **et** **fraus** **hostilis** **apparuisset,**
was named · and · the deceit · inimical · had become clear
(of the enemy)

retro **viam** **qua** **venerant** **repetunt;**
backwards · the road · along which · they had come · they go
(they went again)

at **eam** **hostium** **praesidio** **clausam** **inveniunt:**
but · her · of the enemies · by a garrison · closed · they find

sistunt **igitur** **gradum,** **et** **omni** **spe**
halt · therefore · (their) step · and · all · hope
sistere gradum: to halt

evadendi **adempta,** **intuentes**
of escaping · having been taken away · regarding

alii **alios** **diu** **immobiles** **silent;**
the others · the others · a long while · motionless · they are silent
each other

deinde **erumpunt** **in** **querelas** **adversas** **duces,**
thereafter · they burst · into · accusations · against · the leaders

quorum **temeritate** **in** **eum** **locum** **erant** **adducti.**
whose · by temerity · to · that · place · they were · brought

Ita noctem tum cibi, tum quietis immemores
Thus the night then of food then of rest forgetful

traduxerunt.
they passed

Nec Samnites ipsi quid sibi faciendum
Neither the Samnites themselves what to them was to be done

in re tam laeta sciebant. Pontius accitum
in a matter so happy knew Pontius having sent for

patrem Herennium rogavit quid fieri
(his) father Herennius asked what to be done
{pf}

placeret. Is, ubi audivit inter duos
would please He where he heard (that) between the two
(considered best) (when) {pf}

saltus clausum esse exercitum Romanum,
mountain passes locked in to be the army Roman

dixit aut omnes esse occidendos, ut
said either all to be killed were so that
{pf}

vires frangerentur, aut omnes
(the Roman) strength would be broken or all
{vis4pl}

dimittendos esse incolumes, ut beneficio
released were to be unharmed in order that by the good deed

obligarentur. Neutra sententia accepta fuit.
they would be obliged Neither opinion received was
{pf esse}

Interea Romani, necessitate victi, legatos
In the meantime the Romans by need defeated envoys

mittunt qui pacem petant. Pax concessa est
send who peace must ask for Peace conceded is

ea lege ut omnes sub iugum
with this law that all under the yoke
(condition)

traducerentur. Itaque paludamenta consulibus
would be led Therefore (their) scarlet cloaks off the consuls

detracta, ipsique primi sub iugum missi,
(were) taken and they as the first under the yoke were sent

deinde singulae legiones. Circumstabant armati
thereafter one by one the legions around stood armed

hostes exprobrantes illudentesque, Romanis
the enemies reproaching and mocking to the Romans

e saltu egressis lux ipsa morte
from the defile having come out the light itself than death

tristior fuit. Pudor fugere colloquia et coetus
sadder was shame to flee conversations and the company
{pf}

hominum cogebat. Sero Romam ingressi
of people compelled (them) At a late hour Rome entered

sunt et se in suis quisque aedibus
they are and themselves in their each houses
(they have)

abdiderunt.
they have hidden

Chapter VIII

PUBLIUS VALERIUS LAEVINUS ET PYRRHUS REX
Publius   Valerius   Laevinus   and   Pyrrhus   King

Tarentinis **quod** **Romanorum** **legatis**
On the people of Tarente   because   of the Romans   to the envoys

iniuriam **fecissent,** **bellum** **indictum** **est.** **Quibus**
wrong   they had done   war   declared   is   Whom
                                        (has been)   (To them)

auxilio **venit** **Pyrrhus,** **rex** **Epirotarum** **qui**
in support   came   Pyrrhus   the king   of the Epirotes   who

genus **ab** **Achille** **ducebat.** **Contra** **Pyrrhum**
(his) kind   from   Achilles   traced back   Against   Pyrrhus
(ancestry)

missus **est** **consul** **Laevinus,** **qui,** **cum** **exploratores**
sent   is   the consul   Laevinus   who   when   spies
      (was)

regis **cepisset,** **iussit** **eos** **per** **castra**
of the king   he had taken   ordered   them   through   the camp
                             {pf}

Romana circumduci, tumque incolumes dimitti,
Roman to be led around and then unharmed to be sent away

ut ea quae vidissent Pyrrho
in order that the things which they had seen to Pyrrhus

renuntiarent. Mox commissa pugna, cum
they would report Shortly having been joined battle when

iam hostes pedem referrent, rex elephantos
already the enemies the foot brought back the king elephants
withdrew

in Romanorum agmen agi iussit;
into of the Romans the battle line to be chased ordered
{pf}

tuncque mutata est proelii fortuna. Romanos
en then changed is of battle the fortune The Romans
(has)

vastorum corporum moles, terribilisque
of huge of bodies the mass and the terrible

superadstantium armatorum species turbavit.
standing upon (them) of the armed men sight confounded

Equi etiam ad conspectum et odorem
The horses also at the sight and the smell

belluarum — of the beasts
exterriti, — terrified
sessores — those sitting (upon them)
aut — either

excutiebant, — threw off
aut — or
secum — with themselves
in — in
fugam — flight
abripiebant. — carried off

Nox — The night
proelio — to the battle
finem — an end
fecit. — made (put)

Pyrrhus — Pyrrhus
captivos — the captives
Romanos — Roman
summo — in highest
honore — honour
habuit; — held {pf}

occisos — the fallen
sepelivit. — he buried {pf}
Eos — which (them)
cum — when
cerneret — he saw

adverso — towards wounded in front
vulnere — wound
et — and
truci — with a fierce {trux5}
vultu — face
etiam — even
mortuos — (while) dead

iacere, — lie down
manus — the hands
ad — to(wards)
caelum — heaven
tulisse — to have elevated

dicitur — he is said (told)
cum — with
hac — this
voce. — word
"Ego — I
talibus — with such
viris — men

brevi — in a short (time)
orbem — the circle
terrarum — of lands the earth
subegissem." — would have conquered {plqf subigo}

Deinde **ad** **urbem** **Romam** **magnis** **itineribus**
Thereupon to the city Rome great roads (marches)

contendit: **omnia** **igne** **et** **ferro** **vastavit,** **ad**
he hastened everything with fire and iron he destroyed {pf} at

vicesimum **ab** **urbe** **lapidem** **castra** **posuit.**
the twentieth from the City (mile)stone camp he pitched {pf}

Pyrrho **obviam** **venit** **Laevinus** **cum** **novo** **exercitu;**
Pyrrhus to meet came Laevinus with a new army

quo **viso** **rex** **ait** **sibi** **eamdem**
whom having seen the king said (that) for him the same

adversus **Romanos** **esse** **fortunam,** **quam** **Herculi**
against the Romans to be fate which (as) for Hercules

adversus **hydram,** **cui** **tot** **capita**
against the Hydra to whom so many heads

renascebantur, **quot** **praecisa** **fuerant.** **Deinde** **in**
were born again as cut off had been thereupon to

Campaniam **se** **recepit;** **missos** **a** **senatu**
Campania himseself he withdrew{pf} sent by the Senate

de   **redimendis**   **captivis**   **legatos**
about   to be ransomed   of the prisoners   envoys
about the ransoming of the prisoners (gerundium)

honorifice   **excepit;**   **captivos**   **sine**   **pretio**
honorably   he received   the prisoners   without   price
             {pf}   (ransom)

reddidit,   **ut**   **Romani,**   **cognita**   **iam**   **eius**
he gave back   so that   the Romans   having known   already   his
  {pf}

virtute,   **cognoscerent**   **etiam**   **liberalitatem.**
courage   came to know   also   (his) generosity

Erat   **Pyrrho**   **utpote**   **magno**   **et**   **forti**   **viro**
There was   for Pyrrhus   such as befits   a great   and   strong   man
      Pyrrhus had

mitis   **ac**   **placabilis**   **animus.**   **Solet**   **enim**   **magni**
a gentle   and   easily appeased   soul   usually   For   of a great

animi   **comes**   **esse**   **clementia.**   **Eius**   **humanitatem**
soul   companion   to be   clemency   his   humaneness
                    (is)

experti   **sunt**   **Tarentini:**   **ei**   **scilicet,**   **cum**
experienced   are   the people of Tarente   to him   indeed   when
         (have)

sero   **intellexissent**   **se**   **pro**
(too) late   they had understood   themselves   instead of
                     that they had received

socio dominum accepisse, sortem suam liberis
an ally / a lord / to have received / lot / their / free
that they had received / (loud)

vocibus querebantur, et de Pyrrho multa
with voices / protested / and / about / Pyrrhus / many things

temere effutiebant, maxime ubi vino
bluntly / they blurted out / mostly / where / by wine
(when)

incaluerant. Itaque arcessiti ad regem sunt
they were heated / Therefore / been summoned / to / the king / are
(have)

nonnulli, qui de eo in convivio proterve locuti
some / who / about / him / in / a banquet / recklessly / spoken

fuerant; sed periculum simplex confessio culpae
were / but / the danger / simple / confesion / of guilt
(had) / (plain)

discussit. Nam cum rex percontatus fuisset an
dispelled / For / when / the king / inquired / was / if
{pf discutio} / (had)

ea quae ad aures suas pervenerant, dixissent?
the things / which / to / ears / his / had come / they had said

"Et haec diximus, inquiunt, rex; et nisi
and / these things / we have said / they said / o king / and / if not

vinum defecisset, longe plura et graviora
the wine had been wanting long more and more serious
(by far)

dicturi fuimus." Pyrrhus qui malebat vini,
to say we had been Pyrrhus who liked more of the wine

quam hominum eam culpam videri, subridens eos
than of the men that guilt to seem smiling them

dimisit. Pyrrhus igitur, cum putaret sibi
dismissed Pyrrhus therefore when he believed for himself
{pf}

gloriosum fore pacem et foedus cum Romanis
glorious would be a peace and a treaty with the Romans

post victoriam facere, Romam misit legatum
after a victory to make to Rome sent an envoy
{pf}

Cineam, qui pacem aequis conditionibus
Cineas who peace fair on terms

proponeret. Erat is regi familiaris
proposed was this man with the king familiar

magnaque apud eum gratia valebat. Dicere
and great with him favour) had strength To say
and was in great favour   and was in great favour

solebat Pyrrhus se plures urbes Cineae
used Pyrrhus (that) he more towns of Cineas

eloquentia, quam armorum vi, expugnasse.
by the eloquence than of arms by force had conquered

Cineas tamen regiam cupiditatem non adulabatur.
Cineas however royal ambition not flattered

Nam cum in sermone Pyrrhus ei sua consilia
for when in a conversation Pyrrhus to him his plans

aperiret, dixissetque se velle Italiam
opened and had said himself to want Italia
(disclosed) that he wanted

ditioni suae subiicere, respondit Cineas:
to his authority his subject answered Cineas
{pf}

"Superatis Romanis, quid agere destinas, O rex?"
Having overcome the Romans what to do you intend O king

Italiae vicina est Sicilia, inquit Pyrrhus, nec
To Italy near is Sicily said Pyrrhus and not

difficile erit eam armis occupare. Tunc
difficult it will be it with armed forces to occupy Then

Cineas: "Occupata Sicilia, quid postea
Cineas (said): Having been occupied Sicily what next

acturus es?" Rex qui nondum Cineae mentem
going to do you are The king who not yet Cineas' mind

perspiciebat: In Africam, inquit, traiicere mihi
saw through To Africa he said to cross to me

animus est. Pergit Cineas: "Quid deinde, O rex?"
mind is Went (on) Cineas What after o King

Tum denique, Mi Cinea, ait Pyrrhus, nos quieti
Then finally My Cineas said Pyrrhus us to rest
(ourselves)

dabimus dulcique otio fruemur. "Quin tu,
we will give and a sweet doing nothing we will enjoy Why not you

respondit Cineas, isto otio iam nunc
answered Cineas that doing nothing already now

frueris?"
enjoy

Romam itaque venit Cineas, et domos
to Rome thus came Cineas and the houses

principum	cum	ingentibus	donis	circumibat.
of the leading men	with	very great	presents	went around

Nusquam	vero	receptus	est.	Non	a	viris
Nowhere	however	been received	he is (he has)	Not	by	the men

solum,	sed	et (also)	a	mulieribus	spreta	eius
only	but	and	by	the women	(were) scorned	his

munera.	Introductus	deinde	in	curiam,	cum
gifts	Introduced	then	intio	the Senate hall	when

regis	virtutem	propensumque	in
of the king	the courage	and the favorably disposed	towards

Romanos	animum	verbis	extolleret,	et	de
the Romans	mind	with words	he extolled	and	about

conditionum	aequitate	dissereret,	sententia
of conditions	fairness	argued	the opinion

senatus	ad	pacem	et	foedus	faciendum
of the Senate	towards	peace	and	a treaty	to make

inclinabat.	Tum	Appius	Claudius	senex	et	caecus
tended	Then	Appius	Claudius	old	and	blind

in	curiam	lectica	deferri	se	iussit,
into	the Senate hall	on a litter	to be brought	himself	ordered

ibique	gravissima	oratione	pacem	dissuasit.
and there	most grave	in a speech	peace	he advised against

Itaque	responsum	Pyrrho	a	senatu	est	eum,
Therefore	answered	to Pyrrho	by	the Senate	is	him
					has been	(that he)

donec	Italia	excessisset,	pacem	cum	Romanis
until	Italia	he would have left	peace	with	the Romans

habere	non	posse.	Senatus	quoque	vetuit	captivos
have	not	could	The Senate	also	forbade	prisoners
{inf}		{inf}			{pf}	

omnes,	quos	Pyrrhus	reddiderat,	ad	veterem
all	which	Pyrrhus	had given back	to	old
					(former)

statum	redire	priusquam	bina
(their) station	to go back	before	double
			two sets of arms

hostium	spolia	retulissent.
of the enemies	spoils	they would have brought back
	two sets of arms	

Quare	legatus	ad	regem	reversus	est.
Wherefore	the envoy	to	the king	returned	is
					(has)

Quo   cum Pyrrhus quaereret   qualem   Romam
To whom when Pyrrhus   asked   how   Rome
    When Pyrrhus asked him   (like what)

comperisset, respondit urbem sibi templum,
he had found he answered (that) the city to him a temple

senatum vero consessum regum esse visum.
the Senate however an assembly of kings to be (had) seemed

CAII   FABRICII VIRTUS
of Caius Fabricius the courage

Caius Fabricius unus fuit ex legatis qui ad
Caius Fabricius one was out of the envoys who to
    {pf}

Pyrrhum de captivis redimendis venerant.
Pyrrhus about the prisoners to be ransomed had come

Cuius   postquam audivit Pyrrhus
whose   after had heard Pyrrhus
that his name was great

magnum esse apud Romanos   nomen   ut
great to be with the Romans name   as
that his name was great   that his name was great

viri boni et bello egregii, sed admodum
of a man good and in war oustanding but quite

pauperis,	eum	prae	ceteris	benigne	habuit,
poor	him	above	the others	kindly	he had
					(he treated)

eique	munera	atque	aurum	obtulit.	Omnia
and to him	presents	and	gold	offered	All
				{pf}	

Fabricius	repudiavit.	Postero	die	cum	illum
Fabricius	refused	Next	on the day	when	him
	{pf}				

Pyrrhus	vellet	exterrere	conspectu	subito
Pyrrhus	wanted	to frighten	by the sight	sudden

elephantis,	imperavit	suis	ut	bellua	post
of an elephant	he gave order	to his (men)	that	the beast	behind
	{pf}				

aulaeum	admoveretur	Fabricio	secum
the curtain	would be moved	(while) Fabricius	with himself

colloquenti.	Quod	ubi	factum	est,
was talking	What	when	done	is
	(That)			(had been)

signo	dato	remotoque	aulaeo	repente
sign	given	and removed	thje curtain	suddenly
when the sign was given				

bellua	stridorem	horrendum	emisit,	et
the beast	noise	horrible	sent out	and
			(made)	

proboscidem super Fabricii caput suspendit. At ille
(its) trunk / over / Fabricius' / head / held / But / he

placidus subrisit, Pyrrhoque dixit: "Non me
(remaining) calm / smiled / and to Pyrrho / said / Not / me

hodie magis tua commovet bellua, quam heri
today / more / your / upsets / beast / than / yesterday

tuum aurum pellexit."
your / gold / seduced (me)
{pf pellicio}

Fabricii virtutem admiratus Pyrrhus, illum secreto
Of Fabricius / the virtue / admiring / Pyrrhus / him / in private
{pf}

invitavit ut patriam desereret, secumque
invited / that / (his) fatherland / he would forsake / and with him
{pf}

vellet vivere, quarta etiam regni sui parte
would / to live / the fourth / also / of kingdom / his / part

oblata; cui Fabricius respondit: "Si me
having offered / to whom / Fabricius / answered / If / me
{pf}

virum bonum iudicas, cur me vis
an man / good / you judge / why / me / do you want

corrumpere? Sin vero malum, cur me ambis?"
to corrupt But if however bad why me do you solicit

Anno interiecto, omni spe pacis inter Pyrrhum
A year having gone by all hope peace between Pyrrhus

et Romanos conciliandae ablata, Fabricius, consul
and the Romans of concluding taken away Fabricius consul
(gone)

factus, contra eum missus est. Cumque
made against him sent is And when
(has been)

vicina castra ipse et rex haberent,
near (each other) the camp he and the king had

medicus regis nocte ad Fabricium venit,
the physician of the king at night to Fabricius came
{pf}

eique pollicitus est, si praemium sibi
and to him promised is if a reward to him
(has)

proposuisset, se Pyrrhum veneno necaturum.
he would offer he Pyrrhus with poison was to kill

Hunc Fabricius vinctum reduci iussit ad
Him Fabricius in chains to be sent back ordered to
{pf}

dominum, et Pyrrho dici quae contra
his lord / and / to Pyrrhus / to be said / which things (what) / against

caput eius medicus spopondisset. Tunc rex
head life / his / the doctor / had promised {plqpf spondeo} / Then / the king

admiratus eum dixisse fertur: "Ille est Fabricius
admiring / him / to have said / is told / That / is / the Fabricius

qui difficilius ab honestate, quam sol a suo
who / more difficult / from / honesty / than / the sun / from / its

cursu posset averti."
course / can (may) / be diverted

Chapter IX

PRIMUM BELLUM PUNICUM
The First — War — with Carthago

CAIUS DUILIUS
Caius — Duilius

Caius — Duilius — Poenos — navali — proelio
Caius — Duilius — the Carthaginians — in a naval — battle

primus — devicit. — Is — cum — videret — naves
first — has defeated — He — when — he saw — the ships
was the first who has defeated

Romanas — a — Punicis — velocitate — superari,
Roman — by — the Carthaginians — in speed — to be outdone

manus — ferreas, — quas — corvos — vocaverunt, — instituit.
hands — iron — which — "crows" — they called — put in place
{pf} — {pf}

Ea — machina — Romanis — magno — usui — fuit — nam
That — tool — to the Romans — of great — use — was — for
{pf}

iniectis **illis** **corvis** **hostilem** **navem**
having been thrown · those · crows · hostile · ship
{ablativus absolutus} · (enemy's)

apprehendebant, **deinde** **superiecto** **ponte** **in**
they grappled · thereafter · cast over · a bridge · on
having cast a bridge over (it)

eam **insiliebant,** **et** **gladio** **velut** **in** **pugna**
it · they jumped · and · with the sword · as if · in · a battle

terrestri **dimicabant;** **unde** **Romanis,** **qui**
on land · fought · from where · for the Romans · who

robore **praestabant** **facilis** **victoria** **fuit.**
in physical strength · prevailed · easy · victory · was
{pf}

Inter **pugnandum** **triginta** **hostium** **naves**
Between · the battling · thirty · of the enemies · ships
(During)

captae **sunt,** **tredecim** **mersae.** **Duilius** **victor**
taken · are · thirteen · (were) sunk · Duilius · as victor
(were) · (were)

Romam **reversus** **est,** **et** **primus** **navalem**
to Rome · returned · is · and · (as) the first · a naval
(has)

triumphum **egit.** **Nulla** **victoria** **Romanis**
triumph(al entry) · has made · No one · victory · to the Romans

gratior fuit, quod invicti terra iam
more welcome has been because being undefeated on land already

etiam mari plurimum possent. Itaque
also at sea the most they could Therefore
(they were powerful)

Duilio concessum est ut per omnem vitam
to Duilius conceded is that during (his) whole life
(has been)

praelucente funali et
shedding light in front of (him) with a torch and

praecinente tibicine a cena publice
playing in front of him a flute-player from supper at public expense

rediret.
he would come back

Annibal dux classis Punicae e navi, quae
Hannibal leader of the fleet Carthaginian from a ship which
(admiral)

iam capienda erat, in scapham saltu se
already to be taken was into a boat with a leap himself

demisit, et Romanorum manus effugit. Veritus
sent down and of the Romans the hands escaped Fearing
(jumped down)

autem	ne	in	patria	classis	amissae
however	that not	in	(his) fatherland	of the fleet	lost

poenas	daret,	civium	offensam
the penalty	he would give (he would pay)	of the citizens	the displeasure

astutia	avertit.	Nam	ex	illa	infelici	pugna,
with adroitness	he averted {pf}	For	out of	that	unhappy	battle

priusquam	cladis	nuncius	domum	perveniret,
before	of the defeat {clades2}	a messenger	home	would arrive

quemdam	ex	amicis	Carthaginem	misit;	qui
somebody	from	(his) friends	to Carthago	he sent {pf}	who

curiam	ingressus:	Vos,	inquit,	consulit
the Senate hall	having entered	You	he said	aks for counsel

Annibal.	Cum	dux	Romanorum	magnis	copiis
Hannibal	When	the leader	of the Romans	with large	forces

maritimis	instructus	advenerit,	an	cum	eo
maritime	equipped	has arrived	if	with	him

confligere	debeat?	Acclamavit	universus	senatus:
give battle	he must	Exclaimed	the entire	Senate

"Non est dubium quin confligendum sit." Tum
Not there is doubt that to give battle he is Then

ille: "Fecit", inquit, "et victus est." Ita non
he "He did" he said "and defeated is So not
(was)"

potuerunt factum damnare quod
they could what had been done condemn because

ipsi fieri debuisse iudicaverant. Sic
they themselves be done (it) to have to had judged Thus

Annibal victus crucis supplicium effugit: nam
Hannibal defeated of the cross the penalty escaped for

eo poenae genere dux, re male
with that of punishment kind a leader the matter badly

gesta, apud Poenos afficiebatur.
having handled among the Carthaginians was afflicted
(punished)

MARCUS ATILIUS REGULUS
Marcus Atilius Regulus

Marcus Regulus Poenos magna clade
Marcus Regulus (upon) the Carthaginians great a defeat
{clades5}

affecit. Tunc ad eum Hanno Carthaginiensis venit
inflicted — Then — to — him — Hanno — the Carthaginian — came
{pf afficio} — {pf}

quasi de pace acturus, sed revera ut
as if — about — peace — to handle — but — in realty — in order that

tempus traheret, donec novae copiae ex Africa
time — he would drag — until — new — troops — from — Africa
— drag things out

advenirent. Is ubi ad consulem accessit,
would arrive — This man — where — to — the consul — came
— (when)

exortus est clamor, auditaque vox:
risen — is — an uproar — and was heard — the word
— (has)

idem huic faciendum esse quod paucis
(that) the same thing — to him — should done — be — what — a few

ante annis Cornelio Romano a Poenis
before — years — to Cormelius — the Roman — by — the Carthaginians

factum fuerat. Cornelius porro per fraudem veluti
done — had been — Cornelius — again — by — deceit — as if

in colloquium evocatus a Poenis
to — a discussion — called out — by — the Carthaginians

107

comprehensus **fuerat,** **et** **in** **vincula** **coniectus.**
seized / had been / and / into / prison / thrown

Iam **Hanno** **timere** **incipiebat,** **sed** **periculum**
Already / Hanno / to fear / began / but / the danger

callido **dicto** **avertit.** **"Hoc** **vos,** **inquit,** **si**
by a smart / saying / he averted {pf} / This / you / he said / If

feceritis, **nihilo** **eritis** **Afris** **meliores."**
shall have done / not at all / you will be / than the Africans / better

Consul **tacere** **iussit** **eos** **qui** **par** **pari**
The consul / to be silent / ordered {pf iubeo} / those / who / equal / with equal

referri **volebant,** **et** **conveniens** **gravitati**
to be paid back / wanted / and / fitting / to dignity

Romanae **responsum** **dedit:** **"Isto** **metu,** **Hanno,**
Roman / an answer / gave / From that / fear / Hanno

fides **Romana** **te** **liberat."** **De** **pace** **non**
trust(worthiness) / Roman / you / frees / About (To) / peace / not

convenit, **quia** **nec** **Poenus** **serio** **agebat,**
he agreed {pf} / because / not / the Carthaginian / in earnest / acted

et consul victoriam quam pacem malebat.
and the consul victory than peace liked more

Regulus deinde in Africam primus
Regulus thereupon to Africa as the first
was the first leader to cross over

Romanorum ducum traiecit. Clypeam
of the Roman leaders crossed over Clypea
was the first leader to cross over

urbem et trecenta castella expugnavit:
the town and three hundred fortified places he conquered

neque cum hominibus tantum, sed etiam cum
and not with men only but also with

monstris dimicavit. Nam cum apud flumen
monsters he contended For when near the river

Bagradam castra haberet, anguis mirae
Bagradas (his) camp he had a snake of marvelllous

magnitudinis exercitum Romanum vexabat: multos
size the army Roman harrassed many

milites ingenti ore corripuit; plures
soldiers enormous with (his) mouth he seized several
{pf}

caudae **verbere** **elisit;** **nonnullos** **ipso**
of (his) tail · by a lash · he crushed {pf} · some · by the very

pestilentis **halitus** **afflatu** **exanimavit.** **Neque** **is**
of (his) pestilential · breath · blast · he put to death · Not even · it

telorum **ictu** **perforari** **poterat;** **quippe** **qui**
of spears · by the thrust · be pierced · could · because · who as he

durissima **squamarum** **lorica** **omnia** **tela** **facile**
very hard · of scales · (his) armor · all · spears · easily

repelleret. **Confugiendum** **fuit** **ad** **machinas,** **et**
would repel · Recourse to be taken · was (had) · to · machines · and

advectis **balistis,** **tanquam** **arx** **quaedam**
having been brought up · ballista's · like · a citadel · some

munita **deiiciendus** **hostis** **fuit.** **Tandem**
fortified · had to be destroyed · the enemy · was {pf} · Finally

saxorum **pondere** **oppressus** **iacuit;** **sed** **cruore**
of the rocks · by the weight · crushed · it lay down {pf} · but · by blood

suo **flumen** **et** **vicinam** **regionem** **infecit,**
its · the river · and · nearby · the area · it poisoned {pf}

Romanosque castra movere coegit. Corium
and the Romans camp to move compelled The skin
{pf}

belluae centum et viginti pedes longum
of the beast one hundred and twenty feet long

Romam misit Regulus.
to Rome sent Regulus
{pf}

Regulo ob res bene gestas imperium in
To Regulus because of matters well handled the command to
{res1pl}

annum proximum prorogatum est. Quod ubi
the year next extended is What when
(was) (That)

cognovit Regulus, scripsit senatui villicum
he knew Regulus wrote to the Senate (that) steward
{pf} {scribo pf}

suum in agello, quem septem iugerum
his in the small estate which seven acre

habebat, mortuum esse, et servum occasionem
had died to be and the slave the occasion
(to have)

nactum aufugisse ablato instrumento
had got to run away having carried off the tool(s)
{nanciscor pf}

rustico, **ideoque** **petere** **se** **ut** **sibi**
agricultural · and therefore · to ask / that he asked · himself · that · for him

successor **in** **Africam** **mitteretur,** **ne** **deserto**
a successor · to · Africa · would be sent · that not · being left alone

agro **non** **esset** **unde** **uxor** **et**
the farmland · not · there would be · from which · (his) wife · and

liberi **alerentur.** **Senatus,** **acceptis** **litteris,**
children · would be fed · The Senate · having received · the letter

res **quas** **Regulus** **amiserat** **publica** **pecunia**
the things · which · Regulus · had lost · with public · money

redimi **iussit:** **agellum** **colendum**
to be redeemed / ordered that should be redeemed · ordered · the estate · to be cultivated

locavit, **et** **alimenta** **coniugi** **ac** **liberis**
it leased out {pf} · and · foodstuffs · for the spouse · and · the children

praebuit. **Regulus** **deinde** **crebris** **proeliis**
it provided · Refulus · thereupon · in frequent {creber5pl} · battles

Carthaginiensium **opes** **contudit,** **eosque** **pacem**
of the Carthaginians · the forces · grinded {contundo pf} · and them · peace

petere **coegit.** **Eam** **cum** **Regulus** **nollet** **dare**
to ask for   compelled   It   when   Regulus   not willed   give
{pf cogo}

nisi **durissimis** **conditionibus,** **illi** **a**
unless   on very hard   conditions   they   from

Lacedaemoniis **auxilium** **petierunt.**
the Spartans   help   aked for

Lacedaemonii **Xantippum** **virum** **belli**
The Spartans   Xantippus   a man   of (in) war

peritissimum **Carthaginiensibus** **miserunt,** **a** **quo**
most skilled   to the Carthaginians   sent   by   whom
{pf}

Regulus **victus** **est** **ultima** **pernicie:** **duo** **tantum**
Regulus   defeated   is   with ultimate   destruction   two   only
suffered an utterly crushing defeat

millia **hominum** **ex** **omni** **Romano** **exercitu**
thousand   men   out of   the whole   Roman   army
{homo2pl}

remanserunt: **Regulus** **ipse** **captus,** **et** **in**
remained   Regulus   himself   taken   and   into
{pf remaneo}

carcerem **coniectus** **est.** **Deinde** **Romam** **de**
prison   thrown   is   Thereupon   to Rome   about
(was)

permutandis	captivis	dato	iureiurando
to be exchanged	the prisoners	having given	an oath

missus	est,	ut,	si	non	impetrasset,
sent	he is (was)	such that	if	not	he would have obtained (it)

rediret	ipse	Carthaginem.	Is	cum	Romam
he would go back	himself	to Carthago	He	when	to Rome

venisset,	inductus	in	senatum	mandata
he had come	introduced	into	the Senate	(his) commissions

exposuit,	et	primum
set forth {pf}	and	first

ne	sententiam	diceret	recusavit,	causatus
that not	(his) opinion	he would say	he refused	arguing

he refused to say (his) opinion

se	non	iam	esse	senatorem,	quoniam
himself	no	anymore	to be	a senator	as

that he was not anymore a senator

venisset	in	potestatem	hostium.	Iussus	tamen
he had come	in	the power	of the enemies	Ordered	however

sententiam	aperire,	negavit	esse	utile
(his) opinion	to open (to disclose)	he denied	to be	useful

that it would be useful

captivos — the captive
Poenos — Carthaginians
reddi, — to be given back
quia — because

adolescentes — young men
essent — they were
et — and
boni — good
duces, — leaders
ipse — he himself
vero — but

iam — already
confectus — consumed
senectute. — by old age
Cuius — Whose (His)
cum — when
valuisset — had prevailed

auctoritas, — authority
captivi — the prisoners
retenti — kept
sunt. — are (were)

Regulus — Regulus
deinde — thereupon
cum — although
retineretur — he was withheld
a — by
propinquis — kinsmen

et — and
amicis, — friends
tamen — nevertheless
Carthaginem — to Carthago
rediit. — returned {pf}
Neque — and not

vero — indeed
tunc — then
ignorabat — he did not know
se — himself that he departed
ad — to

crudelissimum — a most cruel
hostem — enemy
et — and
ad — to
exquisita — well thought-out

supplicia — punishments
proficisci; — to depart / that he departed
sed — but
iusiurandum — the oath

conservandum   **putavit.**   **Reversum**
(was) to be kept   he believed   The returned one
                                                   {vertor pf}

Carthaginienses   **omni**   **cruciatu**   **necaverunt:**
the Carthaginians   with all (kinds of)   torture   have put to death

palpebris   **enim**   **resectis**   **aliquandiu**   **in**   **loco**
(his) eyelids   for   having been cut off   some time   in   a place

tenebricoso   **tenuerunt;**   **deinde**   **cum**   **sol**   **esset**
dark   they (him) kept   thereupon   when   the sun   was
                   {pf}

ardentissimus,   **repente**   **eductum**   **intueri**   **caelum**
shining most brillant   suddenly   led out   to look to   the sky

coegerunt;   **postremo**   **in**   **arcam**   **ligneam**
they compelled (him)   finally   in   a chest   wooden

incluserunt,   **in**   **qua**   **undique**   **clavi**   **praeacuti**
they enclosed (him)   inside   which   everywhere   nails   sharpened

eminebant.   **Ita**   **dum**   **fessum**   **corpus,**   **quocumque**
protruded   So   while   (his) worn out   body   wherever

inclinaret,   **stimulis**   **ferreis**   **confoditur.**
he would bend (it)   by spikes   iron   was pierced

Vigiliis		et	dolore	continuo	extinctus	est.
By sleepnessness		and	pain	continuous	deprived of life	he is
						(he was)

Hic	fuit	Atilii	Reguli	exitus,	clarior	et
This	has been	of Atilius	Regulus	the end	more brilliant	and

illustrior	quoque	vita	ipsa	licet	per
bright	also	than (his) life	itself	however much	in
	(even)	{vita5}			

maximam	gloriam	diu	acta.
the greatest	glory	for a long time	carried on